About the author

Janet Menzies is a member of the Guild of Health Writers, and the bestselling author of *The D.I.Y. Diet*. Her career on national newspapers has spanned 15 years, working on the *Daily Telegraph*, the *Daily Mail*, *Hello!* magazine and the *Daily Express*, where she was Woman's Editor.

Also by Janet Menzies

The D.I.Y. Diet
The Japanese Diet

Cheat at Slimming

Janet Menzies

CORONET BOOKS
Hodder and Stoughton

First published in Great Britain in 1997 by Hodder &
Stoughton
A division of Hodder Headline PLC

A Coronet paperback

10 9 8 7 6 5 4 3 2

A CIP catalogue record for this title is available
from the British Library

ISBN 0 340 68581 6

Typeset by Palimpsest Book Production Limited,
Polmont, Stirlingshire
Printed and bound in Great Britain by
Mackays of Chatham PLC, Chatham, Kent

Hodder and Stoughton
A division of Hodder Headline PLC
338 Euston Road
London NW1 3BH

To The JTR 'Babes' – Anne, Carol, Jan, Jane, Mary Beth, Pam and Pat – real women, great role models.

ACKNOWLEDGEMENTS

All leaders in their fields, the experts acknowledged here were kind enough to pass on thought-provoking and stimulating insights into how we can achieve the common goal of looking and feeling slim, healthy and well. My thanks go to: Paul Bromley, sports physiologist and lecturer; Michael Desport, Covent Garden hairdresser; Christine Hocking, Pilates teacher; Elliot Lancaster, personal trainer; Deborah Shaw, Knightsbridge fashion consultant; Mary Spillane, UK founder of the Color Me Beautiful Organisation; and Steven Terrass, chief nutritionist at Solgar Vitamins.

CONTENTS

INTRODUCTION

Lifting the lid on Thin

This is the book to turn to when life plays the cruel trick of putting you into your holiday bikini straight after Britain's most miserable, binge-inducing winter in years. This is the book that tells it how it is. Yes: let's face the fact that most women spend approximately a third of their lives bloated from PMS regardless of what they eat. Let's admit that there are times when you feel like taking a butcher's knife to those thighs. Now you can confess: you would kill to look like 'Legs-to-her-armpits' next door . . . *but* . . . you wouldn't want to eat less. In fact, there are times when you would rather kill than diet.

Cheat at Slimming is for all those times. Whether it's the monthly problem; or the sudden date from heaven that arrives at the beginning of a planned diet rather than the end; or the day you realise that even if you did get as thin as Kate Moss you still wouldn't have Claudia Schiffer's boobs or be as tall as Jodie Kydd. *Cheat at Slimming* has the answer. All the questions the diet gurus would rather brush under the carpet, *Cheat at Slimming* brings out into the open. By letting the harsh, cold light of reality flood into the deepest recesses of the diet industry, this book aims to provide you with concrete, achievable solutions to your slimming problems.

Cheat at Slimming is all about getting results. It will show you how to stop being a victim of the dieter's

'Monday morning syndrome'. You will discover how to stop living on impossible dreams of the future and learn instead to change your image, now, today, by whatever means it takes. Those means are many, various and frequently devious. Everywhere you look in the media you will see celebrities whose perfect bodies are not just the result of self-discipline but of – let's face it – cheating. Having worked in our national news media for the past 15 years I've come across just about every trick in the book. *This is that book.*

In these politically correct times I am sure social commentators will flock to criticise the suggestion that we cheat – and worse still, cheat at the holy grail itself: slimming. Well, frankly, I'm fed up with being strung along on false promises that self-denial today will equal a happier, slimmer future – a future which, in fact, never arrives. I know many women, and men, who feel the same way. With this book I am going to lift the lid on thin, and if it means I never skip lunch in this town again, then that's fine by me.

The Truth about Thin People

The first myth to be unmasked is the received wisdom that there are two kinds of people in this world: the fat and the thin. The supposed logic is that if you want to change from a fat person into a thin person, you must stop eating. This logic has been perpetuated to such a degree that it is now accepted as unthinkingly as two plus two equals four. But for more than 90 per cent of all people who have ever dieted, this is the arithmatic of despair. The theorem that says 'fat plus diet equals thin' simply does not work in practice.

The reasoning behind the original notion runs along these lines: thin people are people who don't eat; therefore not eating must equal thin; this implies that fat people who stop eating will become thin. The flaw in this argument is blindingly obvious to anyone who knows somebody who is naturally slim. I first noticed it when I was working with supermodels, watching them chomp their way through endless avocado and tuna mayonnaise sandwiches (which I have decided must be some form of superfood); chocolate bars; champagne; black coffee for some bizarre reason, and of course cigarettes. The truth is that slim people do not eat less than the rest of us. Not everyone who eats is fat; and not all people who don't eat are thin. In fact there is very little real correlation between how much someone eats and how fat they are.

KATE MOSS, model

'I'll eat anything. I try to eat so I don't look so waif-like but even if I do, I'm not going to become this voluptuous thing, I'm just skinny.'

This is the major misunderstanding behind dieting – that by dieting you are copying the behaviour of people who are slim. In fact, naturally slim people do not diet. It is much more useful to recognise that today the real division is between dieters and non-dieters, regardless of whether those people are fat or thin. Because the statistics show that today, being fat or thin has little or no bearing on whether or not someone diets. It is calculated that at present 80 per cent of the population of the Western world either undereats, overeats or fluctuates between the two, while fewer than 20 per cent get the balance right. Let's take a closer look at those statistics.

	CATEGORY	SLIM/ FAT?	DEFINITION	% OF POPULATION
NON-DIETERS				
1	**Naturally Slim**	slim	Always slim, never needed to diet and has never done so	approx 18 per cent
2	**Chronic Obese**	fat	Always fat, never dieted Sub-group: **Compulsive Eater**	approx 12 per cent
DIETERS				**% OF DIETERS**
1	**Failing Dieter**	fat	Do need to lose and fail	40 per cent
2	**Habitual Dieter**	slim	Don't need to lose, but diet or continue to diet after losing Sub-group: **Anorexic**	18 per cent
3	**Yo-Yo Dieter**	fluctuates fat/slim	Alternately feast and fast/ Alternately binge and purge Sub-group: **Bulimic**	20 per cent
4	**Occasional Dieter**	fluctuates fat/slim	Diet for a specific reason and succeed	12 per cent
5	**Successful Dieter**	slim	Diet once, lose weight and keep it off	1–10 per cent

Do you recognise yourself in any of the dieter groups?

Just remember that slim people did not get that way through dieting, and you don't have to either. *Cheat at Slimming* is here to help you make the mind-blowing transition from being a dieter to being a non-dieter. It will show you how you can look slimmer, feel slimmer and – probably for the first time ever – genuinely succeed in becoming really slimmer.

Celebrity 'Stick' Tricks

This is where you learn the art of thin, though I won't be recommending the black magic to which some celebrities resort. Princess Diana, for example, is known to be a devotee of colonic irrigation – basically an upmarket version of the old-fashioned hospital enema. Colonic irrigation is famed for the ultra-flat stomach it leaves behind, often lasting a week or more. Supermodels resort to vodka, cranberry juice, cigarettes, caffeine and mineral water (still, not sparkling) to remain slim even at times of stress. Jockeys, boxers and Mr/Ms Universe contenders control their weight by getting rid of body fluid – sometimes through the use of diuretics (which reduce water retention). When Madonna was in her 'ripped' vogueing phase she borrowed a lot of tricks from body-builders to get that ultra-lean, sculpted look. Another pop star went even further by having her lowest pair of ribs removed, and country singer Kenny Rogers has had liposuction to deal with unwanted fat.

SHARON STONE, actress

'When modelling I had animal hormone slimming shots. They gave me a terrible throbbing headache and my friends had to practically carry me to the doctor.'

But, there are plenty of other healthier and cheaper techniques you can use to get slim without ever having to count another calorie. What this book will do is show you how to get clever. Remember the tortoise and the hare? The superhare – all long legs, silver highlights and big eyes – thought she was bound to win the race. But it was the pear-shaped, figure-challenged tortoise who knew her own strong points – her many friends and relations – and had the clever idea of recruiting them to help her appear to pass the post first. Did she cheat or was she just smart? She got the job done, and that's what counts.

Psychologists are great believers in cheating. Behavioural psychologists who look at realistic ways of finding solutions to our dilemmas will tell you that if something doesn't work, give up at once, and – here's the point – try a different way the next time. It is simply not logical to keep repeating one strategy long after it has clearly failed to work. Yet that is what dieters do all the time. We go on a diet, it doesn't work, so we go on another one. *Cheat at Slimming* is about breaking out of this loopy routine and doing something different – anything different. From a psychologist's point of view it doesn't really matter what you do as long as it breaks the run of repeated failures.

One of the most important things to do is to rediscover your own practicality and common sense. When you are dieting it is difficult to keep your wits about you. The reason for this is this that in order to function properly the brain needs a steady supply of glucose, one of the first things to be disrupted when the dieter starts under-nourishing her metabolism. Some of the most obvious home truths tend to be overlooked in these circumstances.

For example, it is vitally important to remember the distinction between dieting and slimming.

> Slimming is the process of becoming or appearing to become leaner. Dieting is following a regime of eating less or different food.

The difference is crucial. Slimming is the end goal, and dieting is just one means of achieving it. All too often, when trying to get slim, we become so entangled in the dieting process that we lose sight of the goal itself – that is, looking or being slimmer than we are now. One of the reasons why the morning of starting the diet is so rewarding is because it is the one time when we have our goal clearly in sight. Once we get involved in the diet itself we are so distracted by all the problems involved in choosing special foods, reducing intake, self-discipline, etc., that we lose contact with our goal.

The cheats, tips and tricks in this book have an instant effect – they remind you of your goal, and that it is achievable.

What Are Your True Goals?

Setting your goal and ensuring that you understand it thoroughly is the most important action you can take towards achieving it. Yet even at this crucial first step confusion usually arises. Ask most dieters on a Monday morning why they have commenced yet another diet and what goal they hope to achieve by doing it. They will say that the answer is obvious – to get thinner. But is that genuinely what it is about? What really troubles many dieters is what they look like to other people. At first glance that might seem to be the same goal – losing the bulges, getting thinner – but it's not. The true concern is about *appearance* – literally, how you *appear*: what you look like rather than what you actually are. Being thin, thinner, losing weight or whatever, is not the only way of looking good. If you are one of those people whose true goal is looking good, as opposed to being thinner, then there are many ways to achieve that goal that don't involve anything to do with eating.

For example, the truth is that knickers are what cause a VPL (visible panty line), not flesh; it's peroxide, not dieting, that makes you blonde; and high heels, not self-denial, are what make you taller. So if you want to be tall, buy stilettos; if you hate your mousey hair, go to the chemist; and if you've got a VPL, take your knickers off. Easy solutions, and no calories to worry about. How often do we set off on yet another diet when what we really want is not so much to be thinner, as more popular, happier, better groomed, more successful?

The problem is that modern day Western society identifies slimness so closely with other desirable attributes – beauty, glamour, success, popularity, wealth, health and happiness – that it is very difficult not to fall for the myth. If it helps you to regain your perspective, just remind yourself that if you lived in a Polynesian society you'd be trying to *gain*, not lose, a few extra inches in order to achieve all the desirable things listed above.

We are in many ways illogical about our goal-setting,

so it is important to be absolutely clear about what it is you really want to achieve before you start planning how you will do it. If your true aim is to get a promotion at work, then – unless you do indeed work as a model – planning to achieve it by denying yourself food is patently silly (especially if you bear in mind that the brain needs glucose). Yet that is what many of us are in effect doing on those Monday mornings when we start another diet with the vague optimism that the future will be rosier when and if we are thinner.

Business management gurus will tell you that the single most important precursor to success in any field is understanding your true goals, analysing them, and working towards goals that are specific, identifiable, achievable, measurable and desirable. This is more difficult than it sounds: the general goal of 'becoming slimmer' fails in almost every category. It's vague; it is very hard to identify what it means; and, as for achievable, enough said! It is even debatable whether it's truly measurable, as you can lose centimetres but not kilograms and vice versa. For an estimated 20 per cent of female dieters, it is not desirable either.

> So the first trick to be learned from *Cheat at Slimming* is how to set a goal that is specific, identifiable, achievable, measurable and desirable.

This process is actually far more difficult than starting another diet, so I suggest you grab something to eat and drink and sit down somewhere quiet so you can have a good think about it. Here's a typical case history:

Julia's Goal-setting

Initially Julia believed her goal was to get down from her current weight of 8st 6lb (47kg) to 8 stone (44kg). After repeated failures to get any lower than 8st 3lbs (45kg) Julia began to ask herself why she wanted to weigh 8 stone. Her answers were that she thought it would make her look better, feel happier and thus have a more fulfilling lifestyle. Suddenly she understood that those were her true goals, and the more Julia thought about it, the more she realised that the most important reason was fulfilment. Julia at last recognised that if she could become more fulfilled she would feel happier and her looks would be less important to her – certainly that arbitrary definition of 'weighing 8 stone' would become irrelevant (which of course, it had been all the time). Julia was then able to construct a plan of action to achieve her newly understood goal. She successfully changed her job and built a career which she found much more satisfying. Today Julia is more fulfilled and happier. A side-effect has been that her friends think she actually looks better – less tired and stressed. As for Julia's weight, she says: 'I couldn't tell you that to within half a stone, but the clothes I used to wear are if anything slightly looser.'

Now think about your own true goals, starting with: 'to be thinner'. Does that actually mean 'to look slim'? If it does, then *Cheat at Slimming* will show you how to achieve that goal. Being slim and looking slim are two different things, and the look is fortunately much easier to achieve than the reality. Having worked with fashion editors, image consultants and fashion buyers for years I am glad to say there is a whole reference book full of tricks, optical illusions and clever gimmicks you can use which will convince your friends you are a shadow of your former self when in fact you are still every centimetre the woman you were last week.

ANTHEA TURNER, TV presenter

'Exercise is important, but it is more important to make the best of yourself – you have to know what you are and what you're about.'

If, on the other hand, the mere appearance of slimming isn't enough for you and you truly want or need to shed some excess fat, you still have many possibilities available to your cheating heart. There are long-term, healthy and effortless ways of boosting your metabolism which will help you slim gradually without ever having to deny yourself a single block of Cadbury's or spoonful of Haagen-Dazs. If quick results are more important than lack of effort, then you may choose to borrow the 'celebrity stick' tricks like fasting and fluid management – though I won't be recommending rib removal!

Perhaps when you analyse your goal of being thin you may realise that what you really want is to be a thin kind of person. What you admire in thin people is not so much their actual physique but the personality that goes with it – always full of energy, never tired, generally running around having a good time – and that's what you really want for yourself, whether or not a slim body comes with it. *Cheat at Slimming* will explain why thin people seem to

be like that and show you how to achieve their
energy levels.

ANITA RODDICK, Body Shop founder

*'Define me by things other than my looks –
wisdom, humour, a grasp of what really matters
in life.'*

Maybe your real reason for wanting to be slim is that
you think it would make you feel more self-confident
in public. A whole section of *Cheat at Slimming* is
devoted to the trick of self-confidence, since this is
at the root of a great many people's ambitions to
look good.

I believe that in order to change yourself successfully, you first have to know yourself. After that,
everything in this book will make sense. If you are
having difficulty expressing your true needs, check
out the family tree of common reasons why people
diet. It was developed from research into the psychological reasons for repeating and failing diets,
and should help you uncover what's at the bottom
of your need to be slim.

Don't worry if the answers aren't immediately evi-
dent. There are self-assessment exercises throughout the book which will help you to sort out your
priorities and get to know the specific things you
want to change about yourself. The reasons shown
on the chart are examples. They may well apply to
you, but you may also find that you have your own
very personal causes for feeling bad about yourself.
Bulimics (sufferers of the binge/purge syndrome)
are often people who have experienced childhood
trauma or even abuse. Chronic over-eaters very
often have a low self-esteem and use food as a

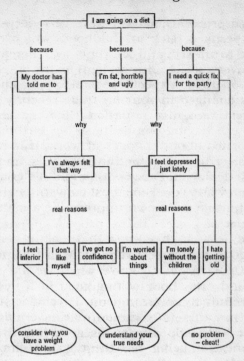

way of escaping from their bad feelings about them-selves. We'll discover more about this in Chapter Eight.

One distinction that does apply to everyone is whether the problem is chronic or acute. That is, whether it has been there for a very long time and simmers along without ever coming to a crisis (chronic); or whether it has manifested itself fairly recently and feels particularly pressing and urgent (acute). You'll notice this divide on level three of the chart. It's important to differentiate between these two different kinds of feeling bad because they have very different reasons.

Chronic problems usually have very deep-rooted causes (perhaps back in childhood) which can be very hard to unearth and confront – and therefore difficult to overcome. Acute problems on the other hand tend to pop up for a specific reason, often something that has changed in your life quite recently. Many people will recognise situations like the children growing up; having one of those big birthdays; or being worried about changes at work. It is usually much easier to spot something like this, and fairly simple to deal with. Faced with a mid-life crisis or a promotion worry, even the most conventional family doctors have been known to prescribe a make-over as the cure!

That is because they know that looking good and feeling good are closely related. We've all noticed how we look more attractive when we are feeling happy, and even how looking good in a new outfit can genuinely cheer you up. Psychologists now believe that this is a measurable scientific phenomenon. Not only can feeling good improve your health and well-being, but those good feelings can be stimulated in all sorts of different and often quite superficial ways. Feel better and you will look better; look better and you will feel better. The good news is that it doesn't seem to matter much which comes first.

For that reason you will find that this book takes a dual approach to helping you cheat at slimming. You will find lots of instant tricks to slim in order to feel better emotionally, which in turn will help you to achieve a physically healthier, permanently slimmer body in the long term. Technically this is termed a holistic approach (covering the whole mind, body and spirit); I just regard it as using every trick in the book.

Give Yourself an Instant Boost

Personally I often need an instant boost, because one of the things I hate about diets is that you have to do them for such a long time before anything happens. So the first cheats I describe are all quick fixes. Rapid these cheats may be, but they are not all effortless. As with everything in life, instant answers tend to mean hard work, while easy success comes more slowly.

If you are impatient like me, or you need an instant inch loss before a special occasion, then opt for the Emergency Rescue (Chapter Three). If an easy life is your main priority then simply choose the Easy Answers that take a little longer to work (Chapter Four). Best of all, especially if you do need to lose more than an inch, is to follow up an instant loss with a long-term programme. Using the emergency rescue tricks will work more or less overnight – but be warned, the effect will disappear almost as rapidly. That's fine. The idea is just to give you a starting boost which will supply you with the positive feelings you need to take the steps eventually leading to long-term slimness. Armed with the knowledge that you can drop centimetres any time you need to, you can relax and enjoy the easy but gradual ways of turning into an effortlessly slim person.

Cheat at Slimming also gives you the choice between just looking slimmer and actually becoming slimmer. As we've seen, looking slimmer can provide the mental trigger to help you to become slimmer in the long-term. For most of us though, just looking slimmer is actually far more important than getting slimmer. This speaks volumes for the common sense of this nation, because currently only 16 per cent of women and 13 per cent of men in this country are clinically obese to the point of ill-health. Many more of us are overweight, but not to the degree that we should become obsessed with losing weight. This is one of those truths I promised you about the diet industry and it is such an important one that the whole of the next chapter is devoted to discussing its implications.

So in *Cheat at Slimming* you will find many keys to creating an optical illusion of slimness, offered by fashion designers, image consultants, photographers and all those professionals and celebrities who have discovered how to manipulate appearance in our looks-dominated world.

The Cheat's Charter

The choices are all yours. You can create an illusion of slimness, or become physically leaner in reality; you can do things almost instantly if you are prepared to make a bit of effort, or you can relax and let it all come naturally – though gradually. But if you are going to cheat, why not join the big league and try every trick in this book? What's one white lie when you could join the celebrities in the big con? Take every offence into consideration and dupe your way to slimness instantly and effortlessly, by illusion and in reality. And remember, if you want to get ahead get a hat by all means, but if you want to have a figure, buy Lycra.

CHAPTER ONE

The truth about Dieting

If one good reason for cheating at slimming is that it is easier than dieting, an even better one is that it is also good for you. Conditioned as we are by the old Protestant work ethic that there is 'no gain without pain', it is difficult to accept that we might actually be better off, even healthier, if we gave up all that self-denial and instead rediscovered the fun and freedom of a life unrestricted by diet puritanism.

The obvious reason for this, as we have discovered, is that if it doesn't work there is not a lot of point in continuing. For some years anecdotal evidence has suggested that dieting doesn't work. Now science is beginning to catch up, and current estimates by researchers put the failure rate as somewhere between 90 and 98 per cent of all diets undertaken.

This is a valid statistic because calorie-restricted diets as a means of weight and figure control have been around long enough to be able to make a meaningful evaluation of whether or not they work. Diets in the modern sense first emerged in the late 1920s and early 1930s along with sunbathing and new fashions for clothes that had no boning or corsetry and therefore did not contribute to figure control. During this period diets were very much a fad, something that only café society would bother with. It was not until the 1960s that calorie-restricted dieting swept through the nation – especially its female population.

.JANE FONDA, author and actress

'I lived on cigarettes, coffee, speed and strawberry yoghurt.'

Not everyone was immediately beguiled by the diet myth. I can well remember my dieting sister carefully weighing out her day's food allowance and placing it in the fridge, only to burst into tears when my father absent-mindedly ate it as a between-meals snack. Another of her diets forbade her from eating anything white – cauliflower, potatoes, bread, rice, etc. – on the grounds that white was the colour of starch and that 'starchy food' (in fact a form of carbohydrate) was bad for you. Some of those early diets amounted to nutritional Armageddon, reducing carbohydrates to levels where hypoglycaemia (low blood sugar) was inevitable. It was probably in the late 1960s and early 1970s that many women who now suffer from disorders had their first deranged eating experience. Although her movie and modelling career was at its height Jane Fonda admits that during this period, she vomited, starved herself and abused diuretics and stimulants.

In the 1980s diets became more pseudo-scientific – but no more successful. A Government survey taken at the beginning of the decade showed that eight per cent of women and six per cent of men were clinically obese to the point of threatening their health. By 1991 that figure had doubled to 16 per cent of women and 13 per cent of men – despite the rise in dieting over that period. In fact, the trend for overweight has accelerated since the 1950s, as has the fashion for dieting. The most recent (1993) Government health statistics for England show that 44 per cent of men and 32 per cent of women over the age of 16 are above their ideal weight, though not necessarily to a health-threatening level. Researchers make a distinction between people who are clinically seriously obese (the 16 per cent of women and 13 per cent of men), and the large percentage of the population who are overweight, but not severely so.

Dieting Made Us Fat

As a nation then, we are far fatter than we used to be before the dieting trends. This is not just a typical example of British cussedness. The same phenomenon is observable elsewhere in the developed world, especially in the United States where it is, if anything, worse. Figures released by the *Economist* Intelligence Unit show that as a nation we spent £70 million on slimming products in 1993, double the amount spent in 1989. In 1992 the Americans spent $36 billion on weight loss. But where is it getting us? Hard factual evidence highlights the *Catch-22* situation we are in: as a nation we are too fat, so we are dieting. But we are getting fatter, so we need to diet some more. The catch is obvious – anyone mad enough to go on dieting under these circumstances is too mad to diet successfully! Joseph Heller would be proud of us.

This catch is not fictional. This is what diet gurus are implying when they blame the dieter, not the diet, for the failure to become slimmer. Time and again slimmers are told that they are the reason a particular diet has failed, not the diet. This type of reasoning has to stop, and here's why: A diet plan is a form of service, a product even, supplied by the diet writer (vendor) to you, the buyer. You use the product by following the instructions, but the product does not work. At this point you discover that what you thought was a straightforward, concrete contract between you and the diet writer has now become a moral issue, a subjective discussion of your worth as a person. The diet failed, goes the reasoning, because you didn't follow it. There was nothing wrong with the diet, and everything wrong with you. In other words not only are you still fat, but now, you are told, you are a failure as well: you didn't stick to it; you lack self-discipline; you didn't understand it properly.

The worst thing is, we accept this diet vendor defence. Where else in our lives as consumers would we accept this sort of shoddy service? Would you stand by and nod humbly if the television repair man tells you the reason your TV-tube has blown is because you are a bad person? I think not. Yet for years we have unquestioningly accepted as fact that although we may show exceptional determination and self-discipline in other spheres of our lives, we must be lazy slackers because we can't succeed with a diet.

Diets Don't Work

New evidence points to the fact that diets, not dieters, are wrong. Researchers from the Department of Food Science at Rutgers University in America analysed several popular diets, including the Beverly Hills, Scarsdale, and Pritikin, and the Rutgers University

finding was that the eating plans were in many ca[
deficient in fibre, minerals and vitamins.

I believe that the whole concept of dieting is a fallacy. That is why diets fail; it has nothing to do with will-power. Statistics point to the fact that the large majority of us are adhering to calorie-controlled diets. Indeed, according to the National Food Survey, we are eating less. Over the last 20 years our energy intake (food calories) has actually fallen by 20 per cent. So it would appear that we are, by and large, sticking to those calorie-restricted diets, and they are letting us down.

We Are Eating Less than Ever Before

The new concern for many health professionals is under-nourishment, as opposed to the previous obsession with over-eating. Over-processed convenience foods, pollution, stress, and stimulants including alcohol, caffeine and cigarettes all make it much more difficult for our body to extract the maximum nutritional value from the food we eat. Furthermore, many of these same factors mean that much of what we eat has little nutritional value. This means that though we may be taking in the same number of calories as 20 years ago – or, as appears to be the case, actually fewer – we are getting less real nourishment in the form of vitamins, trace elements and essential fatty acids (EFAs). Add to this a desire to reduce our weight through cutting food intake still further and you have a potentially unhealthy situation. One American study of dance students (at the University of Iowa) found that seven out of every 10 were under-nourished. To keep their weight

...rs dieted severely and ended up not ...ood to supply sufficient vitamins and

...t Paul Bromley explains: 'First of all you ... realise that just one pound of excess fat on the body is the equivalent of 3,500 calories consumed. In order to diet off that one pound of fat you must therefore create a negative energy balance of 3,500 calories. In terms of weight control by diet alone, that is a lot. For a woman whose average daily intake might be only about 2,000 calories, cutting 3,500 over the space of a few days brings her very close to the area where the body would regard itself as starving. With women there is not much margin – a drop of only about 500 calories intake per day would be enough for the starvation cycle to onset in a slim woman. Then after 10 days of relative starvation the body stops burning solely carbohydrate and fat and draws on protein from the muscles.'

CILLA BLACK, TV presenter

'I wish I'd known back in the 60s about proper nutrition. All that dieting I went through then did my figure no good in the long-term.'

How often have you tried to cut back your calories even more drastically because you were within sight of your weight goal? It is lucky that for most of us the body sensibly rebels at this stage and sends urgent doughnut demands to the brain. For the unlucky ones this is the time at which the danger of anorexia is greatest. Thirty years ago, when the dieting mentality took hold, it all seemed very simple: starve yourself and get thin. The problem is that we have been very slow to accept just how complicated the biochemical processes involved in such an apparently straightforward operation are. Now that we have observed that diets do not appear to work, it is important to find out exactly why. An excellent concise evaluation of why diets don't work is given by nutritional scientist Dr Michael Colgan in his book *Optimum Sports Nutrition*.

Why Diets Don't Work

Dr Colgan explains that there are three main problems with popular diet programmes, all of which occur because they do not take into account the findings of nutrition science:

- They are concerned with reducing weight rather than the correct approach of reducing body fat.
- They strip off vital muscle, which is the major body component that burns fat in the first place.
- They take off weight far too fast, thereby throwing the body into a defensive, fat-preserving condition.

He says, 'The true purpose of weight reduction is to dispose only of excess body fat while retaining your muscle and body water. Yet virtually none of the current commercial programmes make any attempt to differentiate between these three weight components.

'On low-calorie diets of 800–1,200 calories per day, up to 45 per cent of the weight lost comes from the body cannibalising its own muscle tissue.'

So most leading researchers are concluding that

the basic principles behind calorie-reduction dieting are wrong. The science of nutrition is comparatively new in this country and still lacks the accumulation of years of research and experience that we have in other areas of health and medicine. For example, nutritional therapists do not require a degree or medical training in order to practise in the UK. This has meant that nutritional thinking and recommendations have been in a constant state of flux over the last 30 years, from the late 1960s when low-carbohydrate diets were recommended, to the present day, when the Government advises that carbohydrate should be the single largest component of a healthy diet. This has led to a great deal of confusion, even among the scientific community.

The single most damaging area of misunderstanding has been the confusion between *weight* loss and *fat* loss. This is the first area identified by Dr Colgan in his critique of modern-day diets, that: 'They are concerned with reducing weight rather than the correct approach of reducing body fat.' It is because diets are only measured in terms of weight loss that it has taken such a long time to understand that they cause the loss of body muscle and body fluid rather more than loss of fat, and therefore cannot be expected successfully to combat obesity, which is excess fat.

JOSH SALZMANN, Hollywood personal trainer

'You can be very slim and unhealthy or bigger and healthy. As soon as my clients slim, people say good things about them, as if being heavier means you're bad and not in control of your life.'

Physiologist Paul Bromley emphasises: 'People express

their goal in terms of weight but it is the quality of the body composition that counts. It is the
body fat that we need to look at.' This distinction
between weight and fat is absolutely at the heart
of the dieting problem. Time and again you will see
obesity evaluated in terms of height/weight charts.
More recently the fashion has been to talk about an
individual's Body Mass Index (BMI), arrived at by a
complicated computation of height and weight. BMI
is just a height/weight chart by another name and
to pretend it can give you any idea of your body's
true composition in terms of fat, muscle, bone, etc.,
is extremely misleading.

Fat and Weight Are Not the Same

Michael Colgan cites the example of models who have
visited him: '. . . the new look is toned muscles rather
than the sockfuls of pudding that passed for arms
and legs in the Marilyn Monroe era. In vain attempts
to looked toned and thin many of these women exist
on 500–800 calories a day, and have lost most of their
muscle.' Colgan observed that although these girls
would come out ideal on any height/weight ratio,
they are in fact so lacking in muscle and bone mass
that their body composition is actually far from ideal.
He reports: 'The girls measure up to 30 per cent body
fat. Technically they are obese!'

The point is that the term 'over-weight' is completely meaningless. An individual's body cannot be
'over-weight'. A body's weight is determined by many
different factors. You might find it interesting to look
at exactly what composes the human body, and its
weight.

• **Water** By far the major element in our body is water. In *Optimum Sports Nutrition*, Dr Colgan describes the body as: 'A hairy bag of water'. The water exists mainly as part of the major organs and components of your body. Dr Colgan explains: 'Even your bones are one-quarter water. The muscles that drive your performance are three-quarters water. The brain that steers your limbs is 76 per cent water. The blood that carries your nutrients is 82 per cent water. And the lungs that provide your oxygen are near 90 per cent water.'

• **Bones** The skeleton itself contributes a substantial part of our body's weight, and in healthy people with strong, dense bones this will be greater than in less fit people or older people, especially women, who may be suffering from the thinning of the bone known as osteoporosis. So here is one component of the body which should be heavy to be healthy.

• **Muscles** Another major element in the body's make-up is the system of muscles which surround the skeleton and enable us to move around. Again muscle is a rather dense, heavy tissue – it needs to be in order to perform its tasks. The combination of muscle and skeleton is what shapes our body and determines what sort of figure we have. People with a healthy amount of active, strong muscle tend to have a more taut, defined outline to their bodies, which gives them more aesthetically pleasing figures (to get an idea of how this works, just think of Linford Christie).

• **Fat** A less desirable body component is fat. We all need a certain amount of fat in our bodies in order to live. Women need more than men because their bodies have the additional function of bearing children, for which reserves are necessary. For top-class athletes the average percentage of fat in the body is around 12 per cent in men and 15 per cent in women – and it can be even lower in some sports. More normal mortals should aim to have a body fat percentage of around 15 per cent for men and 20 per cent for women. Women should avoid going much below this since it may interfere with the levels of their fertility hormones (oestrogen is fat soluble) which can cause health problems, including osteoporosis.

Fat is generally stored on top of the muscle and just under the skin – 'subcutaneously' is the technical term. It can also be stored in the abdominal area, especially in men. Fat keeps us warm, it keeps us fertile and it is involved in cellular metabolism, but it is one of the less active components of the body, and excess fat has no function at all. This is reflected by the fact that fat is much less dense and heavy than muscle. In two people of the same general size and appearance the person with more muscle and *less* fat will actually be heavier than the person with less muscle and *more* fat.

• **Other matter** There are many other components of your body which also contribute to its weight. These include your brain (which is heavy – Victorian scientists used to carry out a lot of research into the weights of individual brains!), your organs and various other tissues. Even the healthy bacteria (flora) that exist in your intestines weigh several pounds.

All these different things comprise your body's weight, and fat is only one element in that weight. If you are obese, fat is what you should be interested in. The term 'overweight' may be meaningless, but it is certainly all too easy to be over-fat. That stuff that bulges out over the top of your waistband is fat, not just weight. Modern nutritionists believe that we must attack the problem of obesity not by reducing the body's overall weight but by altering the composition of the body so that it contains proportionately less fat and more muscle and bone. That means the bulge over the top of the waistband will disappear because there is taut, lean muscle in its place; rather than because the whole body has shrunk in order to give the flabby bit more space.

How should we go about making this change in body composition? Trying to diet to lose body weight won't work. Whenever a person loses body weight he is actually losing three things: fat tissue, muscle tissue and water. Of these three it is vital not to lose muscle. Yet when the dieter is relying solely on a calorie-restricted diet, as much as one-third of any weight loss achieved is loss of muscle, not loss of fat. Losing weight that way means you are actually losing only just over half the excess fat you may think you are. In order to get a real loss of excess fat, and only excess fat, you need to avoid the various problems associated with dieting.

These include the 'starvation syndrome', where the body goes into defence mode by dropping its metabolic rate and reducing the amount of energy (calories) it needs. This major problem has been observed on a nation-wide basis. As a country, not only has our energy intake fallen over the last 20 years, but our energy expenditure – the number of calories burned up – has fallen further still. As a nation we are more sedentary and therefore require fewer calories. Also, because so many of us have experimented with dieting, our bodies have adapted to get by on fewer calories.

Another diet problem is that of repeated failed diets, the 'yo-yo syndrome' where weight rises and falls within a gradual upward trend. This has been shown to add to the risk of heart disease. It is also associated with bingeing, where diets are broken with a massive calorie intake over a short period of time, which some sufferers then try to negate by vomiting or abusing laxatives.

LINDA EVANGELISTA, model

'I never used to put on weight, but in my mid-twenties my metabolism changed and now I have to work out to stay in shape.'

Equally problematic is the growing trend towards needless dieting. While anorexia is a recognised medical problem, sub-anorexic dieting by women who are at or very near their ideal body fat level is extremely widespread. It is calculated that about 80 per cent of British women have dieted at some point. Since only half the women in this country are in fact over-fat that leaves 30 per cent who have at one time or another dieted without genuine cause. A conservative estimate of the number of women dieting in Britain at this moment is one-quarter of the population. Statistically it is likely that about one-third of those women do not need to lose fat. That means that as I write, seven per cent of us are restricting our eating unnecessarily. Even if it worked, we shouldn't be doing it!

By following the advice in *Cheat at Slimming* you will be able to avoid the pitfalls of dieting and learn other, successful ways of reducing excess fat; improving your appearance; and raising your sense of well-being. Those whose real goals include more than just fat loss will discover ways of raising self-esteem. Those who genuinely need to reduce excess fat will discover the newest, non-diet ways to alter their body composition. Miraculously, these include actually eating more – and that really will feel like cheating. Increasing the body's energy requirement and the rate at which it expends energy will free you from the trap of having to restrict calorie intake. It may seem like a con-trick but in fact it is the newest thinking in nutritional science, technically known as 'metabolism management'.

First of all it is important to come to grips with where you fit into the two groups. In the first chapter you were asked to question your real reasons for wanting to become thinner. Now we need to find out if you are really fat, and if so how fat. Before you dismiss this as an obvious question, ask yourself whether you can genuinely answer it accurately. How often do we go on a diet – a battle against fat – with just a generalised feeling of being 'over-weight' or 'a bit flabby'? It's time to check out your true cheating needs, so fill in the self-assessment questionnaire in the next chapter.

CHAPTER TWO

Self-assessment Questionnaire I
What are your cheating priorities?

The aim of this self-assessment is to help you evaluate your personal slimming – and cheating – needs. Unlike many diet books, it won't tell you that you are a certain number of pounds overweight, or that you should lose so much weight in a certain number of days. Only you can be the real judge of your goals, and nothing can be substituted for an honest knowledge of yourself and your priorities.

This chapter will provide you with many different ways of appraising yourself. It will help you to discover whether you really need to lose fat for medical reasons. If, on the other hand, you are one of those people who would like to be a little bit slimmer for the sake of self-image, the self-assessment will highlight this fact and remind you that cheating and using optical illusions to enhance your appearance would be a much better bet than going on another fruitless and unnecessary diet.

Being armed with self-knowledge and a realistic view of what it is you really want to change about your looks is the first step to success.

Becoming Self-Aware

Body Fat Measurement

The pinch test of body fat is one of the most accurate ways of assessing the percentage of fat in your body and is used frequently by health professionals, who refer to it as the 'skin-fold test'. Professionals use a special calliper to pinch up a fold of your skin and measure how thick it is. The thicker the pinch, the greater the amount of body fat. The pinch includes skin and the subcutaneous fat layer that lies just under your skin, but does not include muscle (and obviously not bone).

The idea is that by using the skin-fold we avoid including muscle and other body components in the measurement – which weighing scales do. This means we should get a more accurate measurement of body fat. Skin-fold measurements are taken from various parts of the body, usually just under the shoulder-blade, the back of the upper arm, the mid-torso over the rib cage, and occasionally just above the hip bone. You can buy skin-fold callipers to use yourself, but taking the measurements is quite a skilled business. It's hard to reach all the correct sites on your own, and probing the callipers to just the right degree of pinch takes practice. Ask the local gym, leisure centre or your family doctor if you want a professional test.

However, you can get a reasonable idea of your subcutaneous fat level just by taking a skin-fold pinch with your fingers. Do the back of your arm first, mid-way between your armpit and your elbow. Tense the muscle (triceps) so you can feel it and pinch so that you have all the flesh but not the muscle between your fingers. Shake it a little to make sure you have no double folds and are not including muscle and then pull your pinched finger and thumb away without changing their position. Measure the width of the skin-fold and note it down. Repeat the process at the other sites mentioned above. To get your average skin-fold measurement, add together all the pinches and then divide by the number of measurements you have taken (3 or 4). Check your result against these general body fat percentage figures.

Body Fat Percentages in Women

Pinch depth	Body fat percentage	Fat level
7 mm / quarter inch	20 % or under	thin
10 mm (1cm) / just under half inch	21 %–24 %	ideal
14 mm / approx. half inch	25 %–29 %	average
20 mm (2cm) / approx. three-quarters inch	30 %–35 %	over-fat
25 mm / approx. one inch	36 % or over	seriously obese

Body fat percentages vary widely in people who look superficially similar – appearing thin is no guarantee of a low body fat. Many models have too much body fat, but this is disguised by their low levels of muscle. Athletes on the other hand tend to have rather low body fat, even though they might weigh a lot. A fit sportswoman competing on the track would generally have a body fat level of around 20 per cent, or sometimes higher for those competing in less stamina-oriented sports. Female marathon runners often have very low body fat percentages, well below 20 per cent, but this can cause health problems. When a woman's body fat falls to 15 per cent or below she can suffer health problems. Some female marathon runners are realising that their performance can also be affected and they are working hard to increase their body fat.

LIZ MCCOLGAN, Olympic long-distance runner

'I snack on bread and bananas. You need to be healthy, not slim to run fast. The media projects this idea that you've got to have a certain physique but that's not it – you have to be healthy.'

When you have worked out your own body fat percentage, make a note of it in the box below; you will need to look back at it in future chapters.

Current Body Fat Percentage	
Desired Body Fat Percentage	

Figure Proportions

Recently doctors have discovered that not all excess fat is equally bad for you. Most women who have excess fat carry it below the waist on the hips, thighs and bottom in the classic 'pear shape'. Another pattern of fat distribution is where the lower part of the body is relatively slim but the upper half – around the torso – is over-fat, giving the body an 'apple-shaped' look. Medical research now shows that the apple shape is often associated with health problems, such as heart disease. The pear shape, on the other hand, is viewed as being more or less natural to women since it is associated with fat being stored in preparation for possible childbirth. So most of us who strive for super-slim legs ought to recognise that to some extent our shape is an inevitable part of being female, and be glad that we are not prone to unhealthy abdominal fat. Apple-shaped people on the other hand, who may be tempted to relax about eating and health because they have the currently desirable thin legs and slim hips, ought to consider whether or not they might be carrying excess fat.

A good guide to assessing your proportions is to divide your waist measurement by your hip measurement. Health experts recommend that the ideal waist/hip ratio is 0.8 or less. For example a waist measurement of 24 inches (60 cm), divided by a hip measurement of 34 inches (85 cm), gives a ratio of 0.7 – well within the ideal. If you are over-fat but still have an ideal waist/hip ratio, this is a very good sign that you will rapidly be able to gain the figure you want, because it means that you underlyingly have the right proportions even though they may at present be obscured by the excess fat carried all over your body. If you don't think you are over-fat but your waist/hip ratio is over the ideal, then maybe you need to think again.

Waist/Hip Ratios

Ideal waist/hip ratio	0.8 or less
Current waist/hip ratio	
Desired waist/hip ratio	

ELLE MACPHERSON, Supermodel

'I am self-conscious about my body, probably more than I should be. As time goes on though, I don't put myself under so much pressure all the time.'

Body Weight

Body weight is far from being the most important or accurate measure of obesity (over-fatness), however it is useful in other ways. Knowing your weight is necessary when you come to working out what your lean body mass is in Chapter Four. Lean body mass is the weight of your body without the fat – that is, mainly muscle. The good thing about this kind of weight (i.e., muscle weight) is that it uses up more calories than fat. This is one time when the heavier you are, the better it is! Because the heavier you are the more muscle mass you have and muscles use up more calories than fat. Moving weight around generally uses up calories, so heavier people often find it easier to lose fat than thin people – a trick which we will discover more about in Chapter Four. This crucial difference between the true lean weight of your body and its overall weight is something that very few dieters realise, and it is a constant pitfall.

Because lean body mass, like muscle, is heavier and more dense than fat it is much more obvious when the measurements go up or down. What few dieters realise is that when they repeatedly weigh themselves, it is more often changes in muscle weight they are noticing than a true decrease or increase in their levels of fat.

When the dieter strives to lose yet another couple of pounds it may well be lean body mass they are losing and not fat. By losing lean body mass they are reducing the number of calories their body needs – thus making it even more difficult to lose fat. One of the first steps towards becoming a practised slimming cheat is to recognise the importance of your lean body mass and make it work for you in miraculous ways, as you will discover in Chapter Four. So make a note of your weight here. Remember, the heavier you are, the quicker you will be able to get thinner.

Current body weight	
Desired body weight	

Height and Frame

The reason for assessing your height and frame here is simply to encourage you to become aware of your true body shape and type. It is important to assess this, because it is the fundamental element of your appearance that cannot be changed. Later in this book you will learn a lot about how to conceal it or use optical illusions to change it but the first key thing you must do now is to confront your true shape. For example, many plump people spend years of their lives kidding themselves that they are just large or 'big-boned'. This may very well be the case for the plump person who is 5ft 8 ins (170 cm) tall, but for someone measuring 5ft (150 cm) to be large-framed or heavy-boned is very rare indeed. Conversely, some women of average height who do have a naturally athletic physique, with wide pelvises and strong bones, can be led into diets that are doomed to failure if their ideal is to have the tiny frame and light bones of a model.

People who are taller than average height often do have a genuinely bigger-than-average frame and they often have noticeably larger-than-average feet and hands. But if you are of average height or below and have normal or slightly smaller-than-average feet and hands, you are kidding yourself if you believe you are big-framed. Wrist measurement is not a very good guide to your frame because plump people very often have fatty wrists which obscures their true frame. Feet are a good guide because they rarely carry fat. It's interesting how much feet and hands can tell you about someone – for example, if you want a fail-safe way of spotting even the most convincing of female impersonators, just check out the size of his hands and feet.

Confronting your body, and actually making a written note of it, is a very good idea because it forces you to face a few home truths. It made me realise that no matter how hard I dieted I was always going to be a sawn-off 5ft 3 ins (156 cm) rather than the elegant 5ft 6 ins (165 cm) swan I longed to be. The hard truth is that being thin does not make you taller, or more popular, or more outgoing, or more assertive, or even blonde. These truths will be discussed in detail in Chapter Eight. For now, just note down your details as a starting point from which you can come to terms with them.

Height	
Frame	

Health Check

As governments all over the developed world become more concerned about the rise in obesity, professional help is becoming easier to obtain. In the past many family doctors would fob off would-be slimmers with a rudimentary 1,000-calorie-a-day diet sheet or, even worse, send them packing.

Today there is a much greater awareness of the problems of obesity. You should be offered a well-woman or a well-man check if you ask for it, and part of the check will include an assessment of whether or not you are obese. Unfortunately this may still be expressed in terms of weight and you may well have to ask the person carrying out the check to do a skin-fold measurement for you.

Your local gym or health club will also be able to give you a body-fat assessment, though you will have to pay for it. Bear in mind that a regular health check is important to ensure you have no underlying health problems that may affect your slimming plans, whether or not they include dieting. For example many enlightened doctors will carry out a blood test to check your general nutritional status – to assess whether you are lacking in trace elements and vitamins that might be preventing your metabolism from functioning properly. You may also have a test to check the activity of your thyroid gland which has a dramatic effect on weight, metabolism and energy levels. This will be discussed more fully in the 'Easy Answers' section of the book (see page 91). If your health check or gym assessment shows you to be over-fat, tick the box.

Medically over-fat	

Personal Goals

To be a successful slimming cheat you need a clear head and your wits about you. The first few measurements in this self-assessment will already have given you a much more realistic view of your body and its strengths and weaknesses. Future assessments will give you the chance to zero in on specific areas so that you can take precise control of what your body looks like. But cheating at slimming is also a mind game. In order to get the best possible results in the most rapid time you need to be just as aware of your personality as you are of your figure.

For any plan of campaign to be successful it must be consistent with the mind set of whoever is carrying it out. In the long term you will never achieve a particular goal if the method of getting there goes against your natural instincts. This is another problem for habitual dieters. Very few conventional slimming diets take even basic psychology into account, and dictate the same diet plan for all, regardless of individual variations.

Psychologists tend to recognise two main personality types – A and B. Both types can be extremely successful in achieving their life's goals, but they often have different goals and go about winning them in very different ways.

Type A personalities tend to be quick-witted but also quick-tempered. They drive themselves very hard, but they can also be equally intolerant of others. These people tend to want results quickly, but don't mind how much they have to sacrifice or how hard they have to work to get them. The type B personalities are much more easy going, both on themselves and on other people. If there is a less demanding way of doing something, they will probably choose that way, but even though their method is slower, their patience usually means that they too will eventually reach their goal. Both personality types have their qualities and are capable of success. Problems only arise when they are forced into an alien way of doing things. It is no use judging a type B personality on rapid results, just as it is fruitless to ask a type A to take things easy. Nobody leaves their personality behind when they go on a diet. So one of those 'lose 8 pounds (3 kg) in a week' diets where you have to be totally self-disciplined would not suit a type B personality, although a type A would love it.

The next two sections of this book offer two very different approaches to cheating at slimming. The Emergency Rescue section is a plan which will get results almost overnight – if you are prepared to be a little self-disciplined. The 'Easy Answers' in the following chapter take a little longer to work, but they require little effort and have lasting effects. Depending on your personality, you will be instinctively drawn towards one or the other. Use the questions below to help you decide which plan to choose. Alternatively, you could become a confirmed slimming cheat by kick-starting your plan using Emergency Rescue and then building on your results by the more long-term approach of Easy Answers.

Question	Answer	Recommended action plan
Are you over-fat?	No	Emergency Rescue
	Yes	Easy Answers – preceded by Emergency Rescue if desired
Are you more than slightly over-fat?	No	Either Easy Answers or Emergency Rescue
	Yes	Easy Answers
Would you be satisfied merely to appear to be slimmer rather than actually lose fat?	No	Easy Answers
	Yes	Emergency Rescue
Is it important to you actually to lose fat?	No	Emergency Rescue
	Yes	Easy Answers
Have you ever reached your desired figure through dieting?	No	Easy Answers
	Yes	Emergency Rescue
Have you been on more than five failed diets?	No	Emergency Rescue
	Yes	Easy Answers
Are you lazy?	No	Emergency Rescue
	Yes	Easy Answers

Question	Answer	Recommended action plan
Are you patient?	No	Emergency Rescue
	Yes	Easy Answers
Are you determined?	No	Easy Answers
	Yes	Emergency Rescue
Do you find it hard to stick to things?	No	Use either plan
	Yes	Start with Emergency Rescue and go on to Easy Answers
Do you lack concentration?	No	Use either plan
	Yes	Emergency Rescue
Is there a special date coming up soon?	No	Easy Answers
	Yes	Emergency Rescue

Use Your Results to Go into Action

Now that you have completed this questionnaire you should have a much clearer picture of exactly what your slimming requirements are. You will have a more precise and realistic understanding of whether you are genuinely over-fat and if so, by how much. Looking at yourself in this way will also have started you thinking about specific figure faults that may be more important to you than overall fat loss. You may also have begun to realise how important your own attitude and outlook are to whether you succeed in your goals.

This first questionnaire has been specifically designed to help you as you work through the next two chapters: 'Emergency Rescue' and 'Easy Answers'. Your questionnaire results will not only help you to decide which chapter is more relevant (although you may want to use both chapters) but they will also help you to put into action the advice you find.

CHAPTER THREE

Emergency Rescue

The situation is desperate. You woke up this morning and realised that tomorrow is the big day. In 36 hours' time you will be going to the party of the millennium/meeting the man of your dreams/flying off for the holiday of a lifetime. Whatever the special occasion, the problem remains the same: it's now, and you're not slim enough.

Don't panic. Leaving it all to the last minute could be the best thing you ever did. This is the time to uncover some modern myths about dieting that few diet gurus will dare to admit. For a start, no matter when you started trying, it is very unlikely that you could have achieved your goal level of slimness by a particular date, since, as we know, only about 10 per cent of individual diets undertaken in this country succeed. In order to get round this, most diet gurus now say that their diets are 'life-long'. To my mind this is just another way of saying, 'I don't expect to see results soon, if ever'.

It is much better to be results oriented and to take effective, fast-acting measures in order to achieve our goals. So by opting for the Emergency Rescue plan you have done yourself the favour of breaking out of the failed diet syndrome at the root of most people's over-fat problem. That is the good news.

The bad news is that you are nevertheless not as slim or as slim-looking as you would like to be on the eve of this special occasion. You need to get answers,

and to get them quickly. It is not particularly important if the results are short term and superficial, as
long as you look good on the big day itself. Therefore
the goal of this Emergency Rescue plan is solely to
help you look great instantly, while expending the
minimum of time and trouble.

Your 36-Hour Emergency Rescue Plan

Your Emergency Rescue Plan takes the shape of a
36-hour schedule, over which time you will take action
on all fronts. When the zero hour comes you will be
looking slim, glamorous and healthy – and you will also
be feeling brighter and more lively. A lot of the methods
you will use are just plain cheating, and are derived
from tricks and tips I've picked up over the years.

Some of these cheats are quick fixes which will
work overnight, but whose effects will also wear off
quite quickly, a bit like Cinderella and that magic
wand. Others work by optical illusions that fool the
eye into thinking you are thinner than you are, and
of course you can use these tricks at any time or
all the time. Some of the techniques described are
real insider's secrets which not only have an instant
superficial effect, but which, if you make a habit of
employing them, will also contribute to long-term
health and well-being.

LINDA EVANGELISTA, model

*'I don't look like my pictures. Pictures are fantasy,
they're hair and make-up and they're about lighting
and retouching. The camera's on the floor so the body's
stretched, you know, and we look taller. I don't even
look like my photos. I wish I could.'*

Your hour-by-hour Emergency Rescue Plan Count-down is described in detail at the end of this chapter. Following it is simple. But don't be tempted to rush ahead now; like any magician you need to learn your tricks first. Here's a brief outline of the cheats you will be using.

	Trick	Involves	Results
1	Fasting	36-hour controlled eating	Fast, short-term, real physiological impact
2	Fluid Management	Decreasing water retained in body	Fast, short-term, real physiological impact
3	Detoxifying	Encouraging body to excrete waste toxins	Fast, can have lasting physiological impact
4	Diaphragm Release	Self-massage technique	Instant, can be long-term, real physiological impact
5	Skin Care	Exfoliation, beauty treatments	Immediate, lasting if maintained, superficial and minor physiological impact
6	Mini Make-Over	Image tips	Instant, superficial
7	Optical Illusions	Fashion advice	Instant, superficial
8	Posture	Body alignment techniques	Immediate, can have long-term physiological effects

Fasting

Prepare yourself for the most controversial truth in this book: crash dieting is not always a bad thing. The conventional wisdom these days is to criticise vigorously the very thought of last-minute or 'crash' dieting. This is because of the recent discoveries about the way calorie-restricted dieting works. On a 'crash' diet the main weight loss over the first two or three days is water, not fat. If the crash diet is followed for up to 10 days, some fat will be lost. If the diet is continued after that period it becomes increasingly difficult to lose fat because the body switches on a famine response, which prompts it to maintain fat reserves by using up other sources of energy such as muscle tissue.

When scientists discovered 'famine response' their first reaction was to condemn crash dieting. While all research was concentrated on trying to achieve prolonged fat loss without triggering the famine response, the other attributes of short-term 'crash' dieting were forgotten.

The major effect – an initial water loss of anything up to 8 pounds (3kg) – is going to make all the difference when it comes to looking slimmer overnight, even if we then regain the lost water over the next couple of days after the big event.

JERRY HALL, model

'I actually feel sexier when I'm a little fatter. I have a crazy diet I do just before modelling jobs when all you eat is two hard boiled eggs and a grapefruit for every meal. I also do the odd panic workout the day before a job, but that's it.'

For a period of 24 to 48 hours only, a crash diet can be very beneficial. A short-term diet is usually known as a 'fast'. Fasting as therapy has been used for centuries by mankind. Many religions include periods of fasting as part of their laws. Occasional fasts are also recommended by some nutritionists for people who are at or near their correct level of fatness. Many film stars and models use fasting to mantain their ideal shape in this way. Naturopaths and many other therapists consider fasting to be cleansing, and an excellent boost for overall health. So without bothering to diet you will be able to get results your friends will envy by following a 'cheating' regime just for special occasions.

The most important functions of fasting are: to make you temporarily slimmer by causing water loss and easing fluid retention, and to reduce abdominal bloating caused by poor digestion. On the 36-Hour Emergency Rescue you will be undertaking a partial fast over a day and a half. The first day of your partial fast will be aimed at stimulating your metabolism and encouraging the excretion of waste matter and fluid by-products of metabolism. You will be allowed to eat and drink, but only foods and fluids that are extremely high in vitamins, minerals and trace elements, such as plenty of fresh fruit and vegetables, and lots of water and juice. On Day Two you will be permitted no food at all until late evening – perfect for those who have a dinner date or dance. This second fast allows the body to concentrate on the work started the previous day, so that by evening you will have lost excess fluid. If your normal diet does not provide you with a good level of vitamins and minerals, you will probably notice that you feel more awake and energetic. Your stomach will be empty, and therefore flat. You will generally feel and look leaner and less bloated.

JOAN COLLINS, actress

'The simplest way to get a flat, firm tummy is to stop eating for a day. If I feel the need I will fast for a day or stop eating an evening meal if necessary.'

Apart from the cleansing, detoxifying effect of a fast, the loss of the water is very helpful for people who chronically suffer from excess water (fluid retention or oedema). So many women suffer from fluid retention – especially during the second half of the menstrual cycle – that eliminating excess water is often all that is required to achieve the goal figure.

And for those in a hurry, losing water is how you succeed in looking slimmer overnight, even if the fat takes a little longer to shift. So eliminating excess water through fasting and fluid management will be one of the key techniques you use for getting thinner in 36 hours.

The '36-Hour Fast' is fully described at the end of the chapter (see page 84) but here is a brief outline to give you an idea of what you will be undertaking. Remember that it is most effective if you combine it with all the other elements of the 36-Hour Emergency Rescue Plan, so don't start the fast until you have understood how it fits into the Countdown schedule.

	TIME	FOOD	DRINK
DAY 1	First thing	nil	Glass of hot water, with a few tbsp of apple cider vinegar; add a little honey to taste
	Breakfast	6–8 stewed prunes in orange juice (hot or cold) sprinkled with tsp (5ml) sunflower seeds/pine kernels	Glass of grapefruit juice
	Morning	nil	Still mineral water; no tea/coffee/cola drinks.

	TIME	FOOD	DRINK
	Lunch	4 oz (100g) poached salmon in parsley sauce with steamed broccoli; serve with a salad of fresh raw spinach leaves, dandelion leaves (substitute endive, rocket or lamb's lettuce) watercress, and tomato. See Countdown (page 85) for recipe.	Still mineral water
	Dinner	Fresh fruit salad of one orange, one banana, six chunks of watermelon or pineapple, sprinkled with 2 oz (50g) low-fat plain unsweetened yoghurt and 2 oz (50g) chopped dates and figs.	
DAY 2	First thing	nil	Glass of hot water, with a few tbsp of apple cider vinegar; add a little honey to taste
	Breakfast	nil	Still mineral water
	Lunch	nil	Fruit juice (tomato, vegetable or grapefruit)
	Evening	Pre-party drink protection formula – banana mashed in 2 or 3 oz (50–75g) low-fat yoghurt (see page 89).	

The partial fast regime contained in the Emergency Rescue Plan will have a real – though short-term – impact on your body. You can expect to lose between 4 and 8 pounds (1.5–3 kg) of weight in water more or less overnight. This will be visible in figure improvements. Your stomach will be flatter and bulges over your hips and on your thighs will be reduced. You will probably also notice that your rings feel looser and shoes less tight. But as a confirmed slimming con-artist, you have many more ruses available to you – many of which are total subterfuge, relying purely on optical illusions to make you look slimmer. Just read on to discover how to become a consummate confidence trickster in the art of thin.

Fluid Management

Once you discover how to use fasting effectively you will find that you are taking control of your own body. For me personally, the ability to be able to take charge of what is happening to my figure – including the knowledge that I can do something about problems like pre-menstrual oedema – is the most satisfying part of cheating at slimming.

I eat exactly what I want, but if I feel bloated for some reason I do a partial fast for just a day and a half and that's all it takes. The frustrating thing about conventional diets is how few of them take into account the fact that the weight, appearance and composition of the body are constantly fluctuating – in men as well as in women. There are many reasons for this fluctuation: fluid levels; hormones; temperature; changes in metabolism; digestion processes; even altitude, air pressure and climate. These fluctuations rarely have any relationship to the body's basal level of fat, but they can be very visible (especially hormonal and hydration changes), and therefore very upsetting for those wishing to be slim.

Diets never take into account the fact that even those of us who are basically slim still have 'fat days'. The vast majority of those days are affected by fluid retention. Someone who perpetually feels podgy, plump and bloated may assume they are over-fat, when in fact they are over-hydrated – that is, they suffer from chronic or prolonged fluid retention. Jane Fonda went through this in her twenties, starving herself constantly, yet still plagued by a chubby schoolgirl face and rounded appearance, which she eventually discovered was due to fluid retention.

MELANIE GRIFFITH, actress

eats nothing but fruit in the morning when she is trying to lose weight.

So a vital element of your 36-Hour Emergency Rescue Plan will be fluid management; in other words, discovering how to expel excess fluid from your body safely, naturally and quickly. In women water tends to be retained in the tissue round the abdomen (tummy), hips, thighs, face, hands and ankles. These are crucial areas in shaping the figure, so losing the bulking effects of water in these places has an immediate slimming effect.

Controlling fluid through mineral balance

The amount of fluid in the tissues of your body, whether too much (over-hydration) or too little (dehydration), is controlled by its electrolyte balance, which is basically the interaction between two trace elements in your body: potassium and sodium. If the ratio of sodium and potassium is at the correct level then you are unlikely to suffer from a hydration problem. Unfortunately the balance tends to be rather precarious, with a constant chemical tug-of-war going on between the two. Most of us are aware that too much sodium in the diet – especially sodium chloride (common salt) – causes fluid retention, but few of us realise that too little potassium can have the same effect. Another side-effect of the low potassium/high salt syndrome is high blood pressure (hypertension), and it is interesting to note that one of the first lines of treatment for hypertension is diuretics to reduce fluid retention.

Even a mild potassium deficiency can cause abdominal distension (bloated tummy), heart arrhythmia (galloping heart) and sometimes low blood pressure, fatigue and muscle weakness, and depression. Today, what is called a 'sub-clinical' – or very slight – potassium deficiency now appears to be almost as much of a problem as sodium excess. Over-refining of foods to produce convenience, long-life and novelty products heavily depletes the quantity of potassium present in natural, staple foods including fruit, green vegetables and fish. After the initial Apollo missions astronauts were found to be short of potassium due to the highly refined, specialist foods they had to eat and all astronauts are now given potassium supplements as a matter of course. Potassium deficiency can also be caused by too much alcohol, smoking, laxatives, diarrhoea, diuretics and stress.

JULIETTE BINOCHE, actress

'If I feel I've over-eaten I drink lots of water the next day. I think that people should listen to their bodies and find their own balance.'

One reason why women seem especially prone to a potassium/sodium imbalance is because of the fluctuating levels of nutrients which occur during the menstrual cycle. At certain times of the month, many women develop a slight magnesium deficiency which in turn makes the body unable to retain enough potassium. If this seems complicated it is important to realise that most of the vitamins and minerals required by our body's processes work in what is called a 'co-dependent' way – that is, it takes more than one of them to make something happen.

Potassium is also a co-dependent factor in many bodily processes, including processing of blood sugar and bone-building, so it is extremely important to keep it at the right level. The processes which keep us alive are quite like an orchestra playing a symphony. Each different micro-nutrient, a particular vitamin or mineral, is an instrument, but only when they all play together in harmony can there be music.

The first step in fluid management, therefore, is to prevent further fluid retention by correcting the sodium/potassium balance. The 36-Hour Emergency Rescue Plan is low in sodium and high in potassium and magnesium. Don't add salt to your food while you are following it.

Controlling fluid by clearing excess fluid

The second important element of fluid management is to encourage the body to excrete any excess water it may already be carrying. Over the years many celebrities, athletes and jockeys have resorted to artificial diuretics in order to achieve this. While a mild herbal diuretic can be helpful during the worst of pre-menstrual fluid retention, long-term use of diuretics is dangerous. It is also unnecessary if we use the body's biochemistry to work for us. Apart from balancing sodium and potassium, you can use Vitamin C to help banish excess water naturally.

You don't have to worry about taking too much Vitamin C, which is water soluble and any excess of which will be flushed from the body. If you have recently noticed that your skin bruises easily or cuts take a long time to heal, it may be a sign that you are deficient in Vitamin C. Many fruits and vegetables are rich in natural diuretics if eaten fresh, and every single item in the 36-Hour Fast is either diuretic in itself or rich in ingredients that will promote the correct electrolyte balance in the body. The following foods are most helpful in fluid management:

- **Potassium-rich foods**
  Apple cider vinegar, seaweed, sunflower seeds, prunes, dates, figs, spinach, mushrooms, salmon, broccoli, parsley, banana and carrots.
- **Natural diuretics**
  Celery (including celery seeds), parsley, pineapple, watermelon, dandelion leaves, cranberry juice, vegetable juice and tomato juice.
- **Magnesium-rich foods**
  Soya beans, nuts, bananas, spinach, spring greens and brown rice.
- **Vitamin C-rich foods**:
  Cherries, rosehips, blackcurrants, parsley, kale, green peppers and oranges.

Controlling fluid by reducing starch intake

Apart from sodium/potassium imbalance, and hormonal fluid retention, another important cause of fluid retention is eating too many starchy carbohydrates like white bread, cakes, doughnuts and pasta. Most of us are familiar with that stodgy, bloated sensation that comes after eating one too many sandwiches or blowing out on a bowl of pasta. The reason for this is that every gram of starchy carbohydrate you eat carries another four grams of water along with it during the digestive process.

The cellulose, fibrous carbohydrates (vegetables and fruit) are composed of almost all water, so when you eat them there is no problem with fluid retention as they come with all the fluid needed for their metabolism 'pre-packed'. More processed, starchy carbohydrates – like the flour products bread, pasta, etc. – have a much lower level of integral fluid, so the body must retain the necessary extra fluid while the starch is being metabolised, hence that bulky, water-logged feeling. If you want to lose fat you must eat plenty of carbohydrate of all types. Carbohydrate is a vital part of the process of burning fat. But this is a matter of long-term nutrition covered in the next section of the book. What we are concerned with today is losing water, so the 36-hour fast is very low in starchy carbohydrates, to enable your body temporarily to store less fluid.

For some people the bulky reaction to starch is more marked and they will find they have severe bloating and distension, particularly after eating wheat. This is less due to water retention than to poor digestion, which can be helped by the detoxifying element of the 36-hour regime.

Detoxifying

When the intake of food is limited so dramatically during a fast it gives the body an opportunity to clear itself of waste products that can accumulate during normal digestion – especially if your normal diet includes too many processed foods. During a fast these waste products will be excreted along with the fluid. Many nutritionists refer to this process as 'detoxifying', although the fast is not so much a detox programme as it is a chance to allow the body to cleanse itself.

Briefly decreasing the variety of your food is also helpful because some people find it more difficult to digest certain foods. Milk (which contains lactose) is not easily digested by many people, and other common causes of incomplete digestion are wheat products, yeast and some flavouring additives like monosodium glutamate. Difficulty in digesting these kinds of food can cause the distension and bloating we so often consider fat tummy. In fact, it is not fat at all but 'wind' and water, which can be made to disappear overnight during a fast. For your own interest, note how your digestion reacts to individual foods as you re-introduce them after your fast. You may be able to pinpoint one particular product that you have difficulty digesting. While banishing excess fluid is only a fairly short-term effect – you will tend to regain some of the fluid after you return to eating and drinking normally – the detoxifying effects of the fast can lay the foundation for long-term metabolic improvement.

DONNA KARAN, fashion designer

'To make my favourite detox juice drink, blend in food processor or juicer a quarter wedge of cabbage, 1 red apple, 6 sprigs of parsley, 3 carrots, 3 stalks of celery.'

For those who want to follow up their instant detox

results with some lasting fat-loss measures, try including these ingredients (either raw or pulped into a juice) on future fast days.

- **Metabolism stimulation**
  Root vegetables, citrus fruits, garlic and green vegetables
- **Digestive aids**
  Pineapple, tropical fruits (e.g., mango, papaya), fennel root, dill and lettuce.
- **Detoxifying**
  Apples, tomato juice, raspberries and grapes.

Diaphragm Release

This exercise works in conjunction with the previous methods to enable your system to cleanse and detox as quickly as possible. It will also give you a noticeably flatter lower abdomen. The way it works is by releasing tension stored in your body, especially in the area of your abdomen and diaphragm, and thus allowing your digestion and metabolism to function better.

Your diaphragm is a muscular membrane which is attached to your lowest ribs and separates your chest cavity from your abdominal cavity. These two areas of your body are also effectively separated by their functions. The chest cavity houses your lungs and your heart, where the functions of breathing and the heart beat occur. The abdominal cavity, on the other hand, houses most of your digestive organs. Not only does the presence of the diaphragm reduce the risk of these different functions interfering with each other, it also helps pump the lungs as well as supporting the digestive organs and assisting *peristalsis* (the rhythmic contractions which push food matter through the digestive system). So the diaphragm is an extremely important part of the body – so much so that in some religions it is regarded as the site of the soul. The Japanese therapy Tai chi considers the diaphragm to be a main 'chakra', or centre of energy.

For many years doctors have observed that mental stress and physical problems can cause the diaphragm to tense up, resulting in indigestion and restricted breathing. Now research is beginning to support these views, and even to suggest further-reaching implications. It has been suggested that a weak or immobile diaphragm can actually result in a reduction of the body's rate of metabolism. Metabolism is the process of turning calorie energy into energy for living and sustaining body functions. Although there is little hard evidence yet to prove this, it makes sense to think that a poorly functioning diaphragm could inhibit breathing and digestion and thus de-energise these major metabolic processes. It follows that improving the performance of the diaphragm should enable the metabolism to operate at optimum level, giving more energy and, of course, using up more calories.

Poor posture, shallow breathing, anxiety and lack of physical exercise can all result in a diaphragm that is tight or under-used. Releasing the diaphragm improves the digestive flow instantly – so much so that you will probably hear some embarrassing gurgles when you perform the exercise. If combined with the long-term work to improve breathing and posture described in the next chapter, this exercise will have a lasting impact on raising your metabolic rate.

Performing the diaphragm release exercise only takes a minute. Find somewhere private where there is room for you to lie flat on your back.

1 Lying flat on your back, with knees bent or straight, as preferred, use your hands to find your bottom ribs.
2 Work your fingers up the ribcage about four ribs. You should now be able to feel where your ribs are flaring outwards. This is where your diaphragm is.
3 Now rest your right palm over your upper abdomen; that is, in the space above your waist and between your flaring ribs.
4 Curl the fingers of your left hand inwards so that you can feel you are tucking them round the edge of the ribcage. This is the point at which you will actually use your fingers to release the diaphragm by pushing it down and away from the ribcage. Practise the tucking movement for a moment.
5 Take a deep breath in so that you can feel your abdomen lifting and pushing your right hand up. If this does not happen and only your chest moves, you are not breathing properly. Ideally your breathing should always involve movement of the abdomen. If yours doesn't, you will find some very relevant information in the next chapter about what could be causing you to be over-fat.
6 Now, start to let your breath out. As you do so push the fingers of your left hand down and away from the ribcage as you practised. Use the fingers of your right hand to help your left hand, placing the fingers just above the left hand and pushing down and away from the ribs. The pushing movement should be quite firm and if you are very tense you might find it briefly painful. You

should hear a gurgle and feel as if something has been unblocked.
7 Perform this movement three times. You may need to go to the lavatory after this exercise.

There is a knack to doing a diaphragm release properly, but if you follow the instructions carefully and tune in to how your body feels while you are doing it, you will be successful. For most people, particularly those who are stressed or have got into unhealthy breathing habits, the results of the exercise will be immediately visible in the form of a flatter lower abdomen. Now it's time to move on to cheats that will have a slimming effect all over your body.

Skin Care

I used to tease my Editor at the *Daily Express* by informing him that the biggest organ in his body was actually his skin. From a slimming and beauty point of view, though, this is no joke. Skin holds your body together and as such it provides the external definition of your shape. This means that in the campaign for a slim figure, the skin is your front line of battle. Yet few of us pay any attention to the condition of our skin. Muscles create the lines of your figure, and reducing fat keeps those lines smooth and lump-free, so working out and slimming are obvious ways of improving your shape. But the condition of the skin has an equal impact on appearance – especially when it is bared for the summer or evening parties – therefore we ought to expend at least as much effort on skin as we do on other slimming methods.

JERRY HALL, model

'I have massages a lot. I really believe in massage. I think it really helps clean out your system. I love all those seaweed treatments, too. I had the sea-salt body scrub and the seaweed algae body wrap. I can't get enough of all those treatments, they're detoxing, cleansing and they leave your skin so soft.'

Yes, improving the quality of the skin (all over the body, not just on the face) is indeed a method of slimming and appearing to slim. It is also an especially useful method because the results are achieved far more quickly than fat reduction or muscle-toning. The quickest way of all to appear slimmer is simply to change the colour and sheen of the skin.

Pale white skin reflects more light than browner skin, and a shiny surface, whether on dark- or light-skinned people, also reflects additional light off the curves of the body. The more light reflected, the more the body's bulges are accentuated, and the bigger the overall impression of the body. So a tanned, matte-skinned person will look slimmer than someone with pallid, shiny skin. The simplest, fastest and safest way to lose winter pallor is by applying fake tan, a step which is included in your Emergency Rescue Plan.

Apart from its colour, the quality and tone of skin is equally important in giving an appearance of slimness. The grey, mottled and marbled skin from which many people suffer, especially on their thighs and arms, is not only unsightly but also tends to magnify the apparent bulk of limbs. Skin which has lost its elasticity and firmness also allows lumps and bumps to become more obvious – and if the skin is pale as well, the shadows in the 'valleys' will emphasise them. All these skin conditions can make us appear flabbier and fatter than we really are, and I haven't even mentioned the dreaded word: cellulite. Cellulite is such a major factor in how we look and feel that it has its own section (see page 176). Beating cellulite can be a long-term business, so even if you have cellulite, I suggest you improve your overall skin condition first with the quick remedies described here before you move on to full scale warfare.

Using exfoliation

Removing dead skin cells, dirt and debris from the skin by exfoliation is the best way to improve overall skin quality. Exfoliation is usually carried out by massaging a body scrub (perhaps sea salt, seaweed extracts, or finely ground rice and other grains) over the body. Another method is to use a rough mitt or glove made from sisal or pimpled rubber to massage the body. I prefer to brush the skin in long strokes against the grain with a natural-bristle brush.

Exfoliation has a two-fold effect. Firstly, it brightens and clears the skin by cleaning it thoroughly, which makes it appear instantly more toned and healthier. The second effect, that of improving circulation, is increasingly interesting because it is now believed that improvements to circulation may have longer-term and more far-reaching effects than anybody had suspected. It appears that exfoliation techniques can also stimulate the micro-circulation within the skin's various layers. It has been known for some time that this is beneficial because it improves the blood supply to the skin – thus preventing some skin conditions, and 'cold patches', mottling, etc.

However, it is now suggested that improving the circulation at this level may have a general effect on circulation throughout the body. In addition, because fat cells are stored just under the skin layer, it is possible that fat-burning activity may be increased in the long-term.

Before exfoliating, smooth a moisturising or massage cream over your limbs, torso and bottom. I like to use Body Shop Avocado Body Butter, but you can choose any favourite body cream or skin-improving product. Using a firm natural-bristle brush (most chemists and beauty shops can recommend a suitable brush), massage your limbs with brisk, long strokes always working towards the heart. Don't use a scrubbing or a circular motion; keep to rhythmic, long sweeps with a bit of flick at the end of the stroke.

Many beauty therapists recommend brushing dry skin with no moisturiser. Personally I find that rather harsh for sensitive skin, but you can opt for whichever works best for you. When doing your arms and legs pay particular attention to the backs of the thighs and the backs of the upper arms. Next, work over your bottom, hips and up into your torso, always remembering to work towards the heart. Omit the area over your chest, neck and bust as the skin is thin and sensitive here.

The whole process takes only a couple of minutes. To get the best instant results combine your exfoliation session with a warm aromatherapy bath which you can run while you are brushing your skin. The essential oils used in aromatherapy can actually penetrate the skin and enter your body tissues, circulation and lymphatic system where, depending on the oils used, they can have diuretic and detoxifying effects. When you have finished brushing, step into your aromatherapy bath and wash off any remaining body cream. Remember to rinse out your brush and leave it to dry with bristles down so that it does not rot.

To create your aromatherapy bath blend 8 to 10 drops each of two or three essential oils in about a teaspoon of massage oil, pour into the bath at the last minute and stir in. Choose some oils from this list, or create your own blend.

Stimulating – peppermint, clary sage, lemongrass, rosemary, geranium
Astringent – rosemary, eucalyptus, juniper, cypress, rose, sandalwood
Diuretic – juniper, cypress, tangerine, fennel, sandalwood, chamomile
Detoxifying – geranium, tea tree, fennel, garlic, juniper, rose
Relaxing/Soothing – sandalwood, lavender, chamomile, ylang ylang, melissa

Get a golden glow

Now that your body is smooth, moisturised and damp it is the ideal time to apply fake tan. There are many good brands on the market which have none of the carroty tones of earlier versions. It is helpful to use one that has a slight colour in it from the outset as it is easier to see that you have applied it evenly. Brands I like include Clarins, Le Roc and Ambre Solaire – all of which include sun protection as well. Applying fake tan to rough, patchy, dry skin diminishes the quality of the results, so always make sure you have exfoliated and moisturised first. I like to massage a little extra moisturiser onto still damp skin before I start, which helps to get a very even, natural finish. Remember to use much less tan cream on knees, elbows and ankles to avoid the tan concentrating on these thicker-skinned areas.

If you can afford the time and money it is well worth having your fake tan professionally applied at a salon, which means you will be able to have an all-over treatment. Applying the tan yourself tends to limit you to doing your legs, décolletage and arms unless you are very flexible. When pressed for time it is best just to do the legs. Not only are the legs easiest to do, but the results are the most obvious. The darker skin tone has the effect of slimming down the thighs as well as reducing the appearance of lumpy areas, and it enables you to go bare-legged in the summer.

The overall effect of a professionally applied fake tan is near miraculous. You will look instantly thinner and your skin tone will appear smoother and finer. Combined with the other measures to flatten your stomach, reduce excess water, slim down your profile and brighten your skin tone, you will appear younger and slimmer overnight.

Is it superficial? Is it an optical illusion? If it is helping you to look the way you want, does it really matter? All the tricks you are learning in *Cheat at Slimming* are aimed at helping you look better and feel good about yourself.

Mini Make-over

The quickest fix of all for your appearance is obviously to change the way you dress. Even if you are on the beach in a teeny-weeny polka-dot bikini there are still ways and means of wearing it in order to improve how your figure looks. High-cut legs lengthen and slim the thighs. High-waisted, lower leg 'tap pants' diminish the stomach and bottom. Broad straps make the arms look thinner; a v-shaped front makes the bust look neater. Then there's the size of the polka dots themselves: big ones if you are tall and heavy-framed; little ones if you are short.

Just think how much more you can do when you are actually wearing real clothes. There are so many styles available that many women just give up the struggle. *Cheat at Slimming* is here to show you a way through the fashion jungle, so that you can change those nightmare clothes that lurk in your wardrobe into your best ally as a slimming con-artist. That means discovering how to dress to remedy specific figure faults, and boosting your personal confidence as a clothes-buyer and wearer. First, though, you need instant help to turn you into an overnight success story. There will be plenty of time for a long term re-assessment of your wardrobe and dress sense later. I went to two of the top stylists in the business to find out exactly what things we can do now, to look slimmer tonight. Deborah Shaw runs the personal shopping department at London's Harvey Nichols. When I asked her how I could become instantly absolutely fabulous she saw no problems at all:

- 'Your biggest ally is going to be a belt. A hip belt slung loosely just on the hips gives anybody a waist at the same time as concealing bulges. Hip belts are wonderful because they create an optical illusion that you have this really long, lean torso and your whole body looks taller and slimmer as a result.

- 'Don't overlook shoulder pads. Even though the big shoulder pads of the 1980s have gone out, use smaller ones to emphasise shoulders. They balance out a pear-shaped figure so that the overall impact is symmetrical and the hips look slimmer by comparison.

- 'Put on a really stunning pair of earrings, to draw attention to your lovely face and not your thighs. Team them with piled up hair and a very simple dress that really fits you and let your personality do the rest.

- 'When you are feeling a little plump and anxious to conceal it, there is a very forgivable tendency to try to squeeze into something that is a bit small, but it is the worst thing you can do. Nothing will make you look fatter than bulging out of a too-tight dress. Do yourself a favour, buy a size up, and everyone will tell you that you've lost weight.'

Mary Spillane, British founder of Color Me Beautiful image consultancy, adds:

- 'The single easiest and quickest thing you can do is tone your colours, especially from the waist down.

- 'Wear shoes, tights and a skirt or dress that are all basically the same colour or variations on a theme. Toning colours in this way makes the eye travel in an uninterrupted sweep up to the face and gives the illusion of your being taller and leaner than you really are.

- 'Whatever colour you choose to tone, remember that it really doesn't have to be black. Diving into

black is often the worst thing you can do. You
can see a black outline more easily than anything
else – especially in the summer when the light is
bright.

- 'Instead of black, try chocolate brown or navy or
a lovely pewter grey. These colours are softer
and more flattering and easier to tone into an
overall look.'

Absolutely Fabulous Optical Illusions

• **Belt**: To lengthen the torso and slim the waist, wear
a loose belt just skimming the hips. The easiest belt
for achieving the effect is a chain belt. To conceal a
bulging tummy as well, use a deep leather belt, which
must not be tight. For narrow-waisted, hourglass
figures a belt worn snugly on the waist defines the
figure and prevents a 'fat everywhere' appearance –
but avoid this if you have a tummy bulge.

• **Shoulder pads**: All the top fashion editors use the
trick of keeping a spare pair of medium-size shoulder
pads which they slip into any dress or jacket to make
it hang better. Your local haberdashery will sell you
shoulder pads or cut them out of an 1980s cast-off.
Stitch a strip of Velcro on to each pad so that you
can take them in and out of any garment without the
need for permanent sewing. Emphasising shoulders
is the simplest way of tricking the eye into thinking
a pear-shaped body is slimmer than it is.

• **Colour toning**: The best way to give the appearance
of having a tall, slender figure is by creating an
uninterrupted line from head to toe. This causes the
eye to travel up and down rather than side to side and

therefore emphasises verticality rather than horizontal width. Create an uninterrupted line by toning all your colours. You don't have to wear a single colour, but all the shades should blend together. For example, you could opt for a fashionable chocolate brown as your overall colour theme. Achieve toning by teaming a caramel-coloured jumper with a dark brown skirt. Carry the colour flow uninterruptedly into sheer, matte, dark tan hosiery and brown leather brogues. Or if you prefer cooler colours choose pewter-grey as your colour theme. For an evening look choose a simple velvet or satin dress in a shot silver or blue-grey material. Wear sheer grey stockings (ultra-flattering to legs) and grey or near-black suede high heels.

• **Size**: Do yourself the favour of giving up wearing anything that is too tight for you and do it now. The stretched seams, fat creases and overflow bulges that appear with too-tight clothing will make you look fatter than you are. Also, they are restrictive and uncomfortable to wear and destroy your morale by reminding you that you are fatter than you want to be. Buy the right-sized clothes and you will look instantly slimmer. According to clothes manufacturers and fashion store buyers a person's dress size does not change until they lose two stone or more. Clothes size is determined far more by height and the frame of your skeleton and musculature – things which do not change during slimming – than it is by your level of fat. So if you do succeed in losing fat it will not mean that you have to buy new clothes, it will simply make your existing right-sized wardrobe look even better.

• **Banish black**: Despite the myth that you should go into the black if you are fat, wearing black has many drawbacks. It is not flattering to the sort of poor skin tone that often goes with flabbiness. It presents a harsh, obvious silhouette which can actually emphasise figure faults. If it is worn on just one portion of the body – for example, a black skirt – it contrasts with almost every other colour, therefore having the effect of cutting the body in half and destroying the uninterrupted line. Fashion designer Mary Quant, writing in her book *Colour by Quant*, warns that dressing overall in only black is associated with mourning. In common with many image consultants and psychologists, both Mary Quant and Mary Spillane think that we should be aware of the subconscious messages that dressing in black may have. Mary Spillane believes that when people turn to black for the wrong reasons – for example to attempt to conceal aspects of their body they don't like – the result can be negative and lifeless. She warns that black is a colour that can keep other people at a distance and make the wearer appear aloof. A person who wears black because she feels over-fat and therefore doesn't like her body is really in a kind of mourning for her body, sending out messages that she doesn't like herself and would rather not be seen.

• **Hosiery**: The invention of Lycra has turned hosiery into a slimming cheat's secret weapon. Most people have discovered the virtues of opaque matte black heavyweight tights for day wear, but there are subtler ways of achieving a thigh-slimming, leg-lengthening effect. Lace and fishnet hosiery obscures the outline of the leg and gives a lean appearance, but must not be worn too tight. For dramatic effect borrow the fashion editors' trick of wearing a pair of fishnets over a fake tan (in summer) or over dark skin-tone tights (in winter). Sheer is actually more flattering than opaque, and makes a less obvious cover-up. Gloss hosiery should be avoided. Matte black tights

look best on tall people. Most flattering colours for
people of every size are dark neutral, pewter grey,
dark brown and nearly black. The adventurous can
try burgundy, navy, red and bottle green. Avoid tan,
pale, white and pastels.

• **Accessories**: Use accessories to highlight and draw
attention to good features. Large, bold earrings frame
the face and attract the eye, but small earrings
should be worn by those with short necks. Bracelets
attract attention to good arms and away from the
waist. Rings highlight slender hands. A pendant
necklace improves the bustline and helps to create
a long, lean line.

Once you are dressed and ready to go, it is time to
face the mirror for your last and greatest trick. As
the finale to the conjuror's act you have performed
on yourself over the last 36 hours, this piece of
fakery is the most instantly dramatic, but also the
most difficult. You are going to wave the magic wand
over yourself and actually become the taller, slimmer
person you want to be, and you are going to do it by
improving your posture.

Posture

Stand in front of the mirror and look at yourself. If
you have used all the cheats and sleights of hand
prescribed in your Emergency Rescue Plan, you
should already be pleasantly surprised and pleased
by what you see. Now you are ready for the transformation scene, where you get to carry yourself like a
supermodel.

NAOMI CAMPBELL, supermodel

'Find out what your best features are – everyone has a good side – relax and smile.'

Changing your figure by improving your posture is actually one of the oldest tricks in the book – and it works well enough to sell thousands of home-toning machines every year. Flick the pages in any colour supplement and you'll see adverts showing men and women miraculously transformed from pot-bellied, sway-backed, droopy-busted, round-shouldered tubbies into gazelle-like creatures, all by the wonderful intervention of vibrating pads or some other machine. But I'm sure you can achieve the same effect here and now, without the need for any electronic aids, because turning into the 'after' picture is really just a matter of correcting your posture.

Most of us know this instinctively – it's simply a variation on that old ruse of approaching any mirror standing on tiptoes and with tummy sucked in. The only problem is that it is almost impossible to maintain the 'I'm-looking-at-myself-in-a-mirror' posture for longer than you are actually standing in front of the mirror. This is largely because this 'holding yourself in' posture, though better, is still incorrect – unnatural, stiff and putting strains on your body. Let's go back to the 'before' picture and start again.

Turn sideways to the mirror and let yourself droop. Release all the muscles in your abdomen and let your stomach protrude as far as it wants – let it go even further by collapsing your spine and dropping your shoulders. For added effect slouch your head down.

Now, here's how to stand correctly:

1 First of all concentrate on your shoulder-blades.

Move the flat blades across your back towards the spine, pulling them downwards as you do so. You will notice immediately that you have to open out the points of your shoulders and raise your chest.

2 As your shoulder-blades arrive in their new position, take the opportunity to raise your chest still further. Do this by imagining a string attached to your sternum (the point where your ribs meet) and pulled upwards so that your chest lifts.

3 When your chest lifts you will find you automatically raise your chin and lengthen your neck.

4 Now take a deep breath in, allowing your whole ribcage to lift and widen in order to accommodate the breath.

5 When it comes to expelling the breath use the muscles in your slack abdomen to do it. Tighten those muscles in order to press the air out from the bottom – as though you were squeezing toothpaste out of a tube. Keep the ribs in the flared-out position as you do so.

6 Once you have breathed out the air, relax your tummy muscles only slightly so that they remain taut and pulled in, but comfortably so.

7 By now the sway-back of the 'before' picture will have almost gone, along with the pot-belly, droopy bust and round shoulders. To finalise the move into good posture, stretch your whole spine upwards and tuck your buttocks in slightly.

With your correct posture in place, you are now a perfect model for the 'after' picture. Remain in your new posture a little while, breathing naturally and allowing yourself to become comfortable without losing the position. This is the most rapid of all the slimming cheats, and at the moment you can probably keep it up just for the big date by reminding yourself to lift your chest and lengthen your spine. Feeling good about yourself will also make you hold yourself in a way better. Ultimately, though, we want this dramatically slimmer, taller new posture to become permanent. And that takes more than the quick fix provided by your Emergency Rescue Plan. When you have achieved your 36-hour instant transformation, turn to the next chapter to discover how you can effortlessly acquire that supermodel look for keeps.

The 36-Hour Countdown to Slim Down

Now that you are familiar with the many different tricks you can use to cheat at slimming overnight, here is your hour-by-hour countdown to putting them all into action. Remember to stick closely to the fasting regime in order to achieve the full water reduction benefits.

MEDICAL NOTE: If you are pregnant, being treated for any medical conditions, or are concerned about your health please consult your doctor before fasting.

Day One – 36 hours before the deadline
7.30 am
On rising, drink a glass of hot water with 2 tbsp apple cider vinegar. Sweeten with a little honey if necessary. This is an acquired taste which many people grow to like. If necessary you can substitute pure lemon juice for the apple cider vinegar, but it is

worth forcing yourself to try it for its detox benefits.
Chew a 100–500mg Vitamin C tablet, preferably
Redoxin chewable.

8.30 am
Breakfast
6 to 8 stewed prunes in orange juice (hot or cold),
sprinkled with a teaspoon of sunflower seeds or pine
kernels.
A glass of grapefruit juice.
No coffee or tea.

9.30 am – 1.30 pm
No mid-morning snack or coffee or tea, but drink as
much still mineral water as desired.

1.30 pm
Lunch
4 oz poached salmon in parsley sauce with steamed
broccoli. Poach the salmon gently in a little water
with lemon juice, herbs and wine if desired. Remove salmon and keep warm. Reserve 2 tbsp of the
stock.
Blend 7 oz (175g) skimmed milk with two tsp of
cornflour.
To make the parsley sauce, finely chop a large bunch
of fresh parsley and simmer briefly in the reserved
stock. Add the milk/cornflour mixture and cook
until thick.
Pour sauce over salmon and serve with a salad of
fresh raw spinach leaves, dandelion leaves (substitute endive, rocket or lamb's lettuce when out of
season), watercress, and tomato dressed with olive
oil and cider vinegar and garnished with crushed
walnuts or pine kernels.
Dandelion leaves are an excellent diuretic (as well
as an interesting, slightly peppery salad ingredient)
and are easily cropped from the garden through the
spring and summer. Out-of-season rocket, lamb's

lettuce or endive make a good, if rather more pricey, substitute.

Make sure you don't add any salt during the preparation of your meal.

If you are unable to be at home at lunch time to cook your meal you can make up the salad in advance and take it with you. The salmon in sauce is delicious cold.

If necessary, you can omit the salmon in parsley sauce, but it is very important to eat the salad as it contains many diuretic ingredients. Allow yourself a piece of fruit as well and drink grapefruit juice, which is very cleansing. It is important to have your main meal at lunch time in order to allow time for digestion.

2.30 pm

The next step is your skin exfoliation and fake tan programme. This can be fitted in at any convenient time today, or even tomorrow morning. Remember, though, that you must allow long enough for the fake tan to develop fully (around eight to 12 hours), so leaving it until your bath before the big event will be too late.

3.30–6.30 pm

Eat and drink nothing but mineral water. Chew a 100–500mg Vitamin C tablet.

6.30 pm

This is a good time to do your first 'diaphragm release' exercise.

For a pre-dinner drink have a Virgin Mary made with tomato or vegetable juice. This is an ideal party drink if you don't want to have alcohol. Not only can nobody tell you are not drinking, but also the drink is so tasty that often you don't notice yourself! Also it is packed full of vitamins and minerals so you can go on working on your health and new slim figure even while you are partying.

7.30 pm

Dinner

Fresh fruit salad of one orange, one banana, six chunks of watermelon or pineapple, sprinkled with 2 oz (50g) low-fat, plain unsweetened yoghurt and 2 oz (50g) chopped dates and figs.

If you like a hot drink in the evening then have fresh orange or pure lemon juice diluted with boiled water to taste. To liven it up a bit, sprinkle with cinnamon or nutmeg.

Remember, you are not allowed coffee or tea during the fast period.

9.30 pm

This is a good moment to check the clothes you will be wearing for the big event. As you try on the outfit, remember some of the image consultants' tips. Does it really fit you or is it a touch small? If it is even slightly too tight, then face facts; you still have time to go out and buy something that does fit, or is even slightly big. Remember, nothing is so fattening and unflattering as wearing clothes that are too tight.

Try out accessories with your outfit. How about a belt skimming your hips – this is a great way of making your waist look slimmer. Check the shade of the hosiery you plan to wear; it should tone in with both your dress/skirt and your shoes. This will give the eye an uninterrupted line and create an illusion of length and slimness. By checking your outfit now you are giving yourself time to rectify any problems.

10.30 pm – 7 am

To bed

Sleep is a great beautifier, so try to get a good eight hours in the night before. If you have a favourite moisturising cream or a specialist night cream, put it on as it will help your face look fresher the next day. Eyepads or cucumber slices (even cold used teabags) are good for puffy eyes. If you sleep on your back put a pillow under your knees; if you sleep on your side put it between your knees. This helps to prevent back strain and it also helps to discourage overnight poor circulation which can lead to morning fluid retention.

Chew a 100–500 g Vitamin C tablet last thing. You may find you need to get up in the night to go to the lavatory; don't worry. This is a sign that the fast is working.

Day Two
7.30 am
On rising, drink a glass of hot water with apple cider vinegar.

Chew a 100–500mg Vitamin C tablet.

Perform your diaphragm release exercise. Now start your posture practice. Use the mirror to adjust and improve your posture as described, and try to keep it going throughout the day.

8.30 am – 1.30 pm
Follow your normal daily routine, but omit any breakfast or snacks. Drink only still mineral water.

1.30 pm
Instead of lunch, drink one glass of fruit juice (tomato, vegetable or grapefruit). Chew a 100–500mg Vitamin C tablet. If you have an opportunity, perform the diaphragm release exercise.

2.30–6.30 pm
Follow your normal routine including your usual party preparations. When you have your bath, avoid making it too hot and use the recommended diuretic and toning aromatherapy oils. When you are dressing, put all the tips into practice. Drink nothing at all during this period.

6.30 pm
Check your posture in front of the mirror and try to keep it in place without becoming too tense. If you plan to drink alcohol during the evening – and I can't think of a reason to hold back – then follow this Pre-drink Protection Formula:
Eat a banana mashed in 2 or 3 oz (50–75g) of low-fat yoghurt.
This will coat the lining of your stomach and slow down the rate at which alcohol is absorbed into your bloodstream. Remember, you will be slimmer, lighter and carrying less fluid than normal, so your body may react more strongly to alcohol than you are used to.
Another good stomach liner is olive oil, so head for the olives when you arrive at the party.
Drink a glass of water for every alcoholic drink you have to prevent dehydration and slow down your overall rate of alcohol intake.
Before you go to bed try a high-energy drink (Lucozade, Gatorade or another sports drink) to replace fluid and help maintain blood sugar over-night.
7.30 pm PARTY ON!

TERRY O'NEILL, photographer

'Believe in yourself, be confident and just pretend you're a supermodel.'

CHAPTER FOUR

Easy Answers

What would be the best possible slimming cheat you could imagine? For most of us the answer is to be able to let go and eat as much as we want, but still be slim. A fantasy? This chapter of *Cheat at Slimming* will show you how to turn your dream into reality by using effortless, long-term tricks that will permit you to eat more and achieve a better body at the same time. The secret is deceptively simple: Make your body work with you, rather than against you. Many long-term dieters will instinctively recognise the sense of this concept. How often have we felt – as yet another diet goes crashing down in pounds gained – that we are at war with our bodies? Those thighs which stubbornly fail to lose even a single dimple; that stomach that manages to swell up on thin air – they've become enemies, seemingly determined to undermine and resist even our most stringent efforts at self-denial. The truth of the matter is that when we diet we are indeed in a battle with our own bodies – but remember: it is the dieter who has declared war first. As far as our bodies are concerned, going on a diet is the equivalent of the attack on Pearl Harbour. Naturally the body goes into defence mode, and the fight is on.

The Battle with the Body

For most dieters it becomes a war of attrition, with the body firmly entrenched on one side and the dieter's will-power dug in on the other. First one side then the other will make a push, only to retreat again, with much needless suffering for both. And these are the lucky dieters; fortunately for them, their body's natural defence mechanisms are strong enough to prevent them from falling into real physical or mental ill-health. For an unlucky few, strength of mind can become a compulsion, and it is among these people that eating disorders develop. Psychiatrists working with anorexics and bulimics observe that they view their body as an enemy in a very real sense. It is something separate from what they regard as their 'self' and their attacks on their body can be very real. Now though, there is another way. This plan is cunning, intelligent and effective. *Don't fight*. Don't go into battle with your body; chicken out, become a conscientious objector to diet warfare.

Time for a Truce

Dieting actually prevents your body from functioning fully by triggering the famine response described in Chapter Three, and the easiest way to stop that 'famine plateau' is to simply eat more, rather than less. Nutritionists recommend that the best response to a diet plateau is to change something. The good news is that it doesn't matter what you change, almost anything will do. That is why this method of cheating at slimming is so effortless. At its very easiest first stage – which is stopping dieting – you can get results by doing nothing! For example, if you have a tendency to binge, think of what triggers the binge – the answer is likely to be the diet you have just been or are about to go on. The constrictions of the diet cause the binge, so stop the diets and the binges stop.

> ### BELINDA CARLISLE, singer
>
> *'I now understand that food should be enjoyed. For so many years I felt that it was the enemy.'*

Long-term there is even more you can do. You can go further and positively work with your body, making your body your biggest ally in helping you to be lean, healthy, energetic and happy. The trick is to encourage your body to function at its optimum level. There are many ways of enabling it to do this, not only by stopping your diet but by eating more and better; by becoming more active; even by changing the way you breathe. All these ways have one thing in common – they rev up your body so that it functions more efficiently and more dynamically . . . for good. This effortless get-slim trick is one that will last – without the need for repeated diets. When you are on a diet, your body conserves energy by just ticking over. By following the advice in this chapter you will make your body more energy intensive; you will be 'firing on all cylinders', as the saying goes. Doing this will make you slimmer in the long term because you will use up more calorie-energy.

Revving Up the Body's Metabolic Engine

By making your body more energy intensive, you will increase the number of calories your body needs to keep itself going on a daily basis. This trick means that you will be able to cheat at slimming by eating the same amount of calories as you would normally, but you won't need to diet any longer. It may seem like a miracle, but like so many of the 'magic' tricks in this book, it is actually based on sound research. The latest thinking in nutritional science is that we should be aiming to slim down, not by decreasing the number of calories we take in each day from eating, but through increasing the number of calories we use up in our bodily processes. This theory is called 'metabolic enhancement', and many sportsmen and -women are finding that it really works. Through metabolic enhancement you will find:

- you can eat more without gaining fat;
- you will have more energy;
- you will be more successful in losing fat;
- you will be less tired;
- you will be less susceptible to colds and flu;
- you will sleep better;
- you will feel more energetic.

First let's find out more about how the metabolism works, then we can start on a campaign to rev it up.

NICOLA FAIRBROTHER, Judo world champion

'I believe your body naturally knows what it wants and you should listen to it. Anything in moderation is OK – I do like chocolate, strawberry jam and cheesy, creamy sauces. I take a multi-vitamin and drink mainly water and juice.'

What is Metabolism?

It might be helpful to think of your metabolism as an internal combustion engine. In order for the engine to turn over it needs three things: fuel, a spark to ignite it, and air to burn in. If there isn't enough fuel the engine sputters and comes to a halt. Without a spark it doesn't start. Without enough air it may run, but it will not use its fuel efficiently and may stall frequently. The body's metabolism works in much the same way. It needs fuel, in the shape of calories from food, which then goes into the digestive system (the body's equivalent of the spark plug) where, with the help of oxygen (air), it is broken down for use throughout the body.

Those uses include powering the muscles, just as the engine makes the car's wheels turn, as well as many other functions which cars can't perform. These include repairing cell damage, re-building tissue, fighting infection, and the thought process (which takes rather a lot of fuel). The automotive equivalent would be a car that could strip off its own rust and re-touch the paintwork, beat out any damaged panels, service itself and hire a lawyer to contest speeding tickets. Nutritionist Steven Terrass has a profound respect for the human metabolism. 'There are literally trillions of cells within your body,' he explains, 'and bio-chemical events are taking place non-stop – the whole massively complex process has to keep running 24 hours a day without malfunctioning.' It makes you realise what a fantastic piece of bio-engineering you are, and why it is so important to keep your service history up to date.

Obviously we all want our cars to be as economical

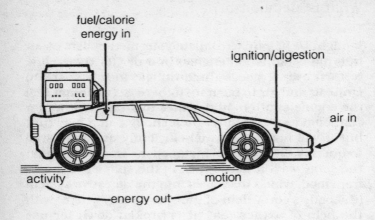

fuel/calorie energy in

ignition/digestion

air in

activity

motion

energy out

as possible when it comes to fuel, but as slimming cheats we want the exact opposite from our own personal engine – our metabolism. Since human fuel is food and we want to be able to eat plenty of it, we don't want our metabolism to be economical. We want our metabolism to be very intensive on fuel, so that we keep on having to refill the tank – with lovely food! That means turning our body into the equivalent of a high-performance sportscar. The metabolism of the long-term dieter, on the other hand, is like a very economical car – it needs hardly any fuel at all to keep it going. Of course, as any motoring buff will tell you, you don't get high performance from an economical car.

The same is true of a long-term dieter. They tend

to lack energy, to be susceptible to colds, sometimes they may actually be slower moving and less active. This chapter will show you how to turn your personal 'engine' into that of a gas-guzzling super car. A confirmed cheater at slimming will end up with a metabolism like a high-powered sportscar doing 100 kph down the motorway. By comparison, the perpetual dieter is an old banger chugging along the slow lane in a cloud of exhaust.

Metabolism Boosting

In this chapter you will discover lots of ways of boosting your metabolism, many of them very simple. Professor Robert Thayer, author of *The Origin of Everyday Moods*, provides a practical example of metabolism enhancement: 'If you get up from a chair and walk around a whole host of things happen. Your metabolism rises, your cardiovascular and respiratory system go into action and neuro-transmitters shift in the brain – your body is generally aroused. The body thrives on oxygen and so getting higher levels can make you feel good. As your core temperature rises and your muscles are warmed it stimulates the hypothalamus in the brain to give you a relaxed feeling.'

DEMI MOORE, film star

works out vigorously; also practises mountain walking and free mountain climbing.

It's as easy as that – just a little extra movement

and you are on your way to achieving a higher metabolism. To boost the metabolism as efficiently as possible it is important to work on all its three main elements, each of which has its own scientific name. Here's a reminder of the three main elements together with the scientific terms which relate to them:

- **Fuel In and Out** Calorie energy taken in as food and put out as activity; the rate at which this turns over is known as the Basal Metabolic Rate (BMR).
- **Air** Oxygen is vital for metabolic processes to take place, including the increased oxygen requirements caused by exercise – known as the Physical Activity Requirement (PAR).
- **Ignition** The 'spark' is the digestive process, known as Specific Dynamic Effect (SDE).

Just as a car's engine can run better or worse depending on the quality of its fuel, whether or not it has been serviced, and whether the engine is letting in enough air, so the body's metabolism can run faster or slower. The level at which it is running is known as the Overall Metabolic Rate (OMR), which is comprised of all the elements – fuel, air and ignition. The higher the level at which the OMR is running, the more energy intensive it is and the more fuel it needs. That's good news for cheats like us who want to eat as much as we like and still be slim.

If the OMR falls, then it needs fewer calories to fuel it. Several things reduce the OMR:
- dieting (by triggering the famine response);
- not using good quality fuel (food);
- a very sedentary lifestyle;

- **not breathing properly.**

The table below gives some examples of average OMRs among different groups of people:

Overall Metabolic Rates			
MEN	OMR in calories	WOMEN	OMR in calories
Activity level		**Activity level**	
Small, ultra-sedentary (couch potato)	2,100	Habitual dieter, thin, little activity	1,400
Office worker, no physical recreation	2,400	Office worker, no physical recreation	1,800
Office worker with occasional outdoor hobbies	2,500	Office worker with occasional outdoor hobbies	2,000
Frequent exerciser	2,900	Frequent exerciser	2,200
Serious sportsman	3,200	Serious sportswoman	2,500
Manual labourer	3,500	Pregnant	2,500
Athlete	3,500	Breastfeeding	2,700

As you can see, these rates can vary by around 1,000 calories a day – the average dieter's whole daily allowance – making it very obvious why increasing your OMR by boosting your metabolism can be more effective than dieting. In order to be slim the cheat's way, we want to make sure that all the elements which go to make up the OMR are working effectively. To transform the metabolism into an energy-intensive high-performance engine we need to boost the activity of all three elements of the OMR: fuel, air, and ignition/digestion. Here's a brief outline of what you will be doing to achieve this on the Metabolism Booster Plan:

Fuel-burning Boosters
- **Eating differently** – increasing intake of certain foods to boost the BMR (Basal Metabolic Rate).
- **Changing eating patterns** – eating early and frequently to increase calorie-burning.
- **Super-nutrition** – adding vitamins and minerals that will speed up fuel use.

Digestion/Ignition Boosting
- **Eating more** – increasing the rate at which calories are used for digestive processes.

Air Intake Boosting
- **Breathing better** – permitting metabolic processes to work faster by supplying sufficient oxygen.
- **Improving posture** – to encourage breathing and increase energy requirements.
- **Increasing exercise** – to increase requirement for oxygen, and increase metabolism by building muscle and burning fuel.

Your Personal OMR

It is a useful exercise to find out your own metabolic rate because it gives you an idea of just how much you could boost your OMR (Overall Metabolic Rate) to become slimmer, fitter and more energetic without having to eat less. Even before we put into action plans to raise the OMR figure, you will certainly find your present level very revealing. If it is very low, you can see why dieting is such a mistake. For example: 1,500 calories per day is really about the minimum to which anyone should reduce their food intake. But if your OMR is already only about 1,500 to 1,800 calories, then cutting your calorie intake down to this figure means that you are not really eating less than your body requires – which is what calorie-controlled dieting is meant to be all about. Now you can see exactly why your diets have been failing.

Dr Ann Walker, senior lecturer in human nutrition at Reading University, believes that reduction in OMR due to lack of exercise is one of the main problems for dieters today. She has said, 'We are now so sedentary that we cannot eat sufficient food to gain the micronutrients we require without getting fatter.' So instead of falling into the trap of continuing to cut food intake, we are going to cheat by raising the amount of food energy your body uses up – by boosting your OMR.

Finding Your Personal OMR

• Step One: Calculate your Basal Metabolic Rate (BMR)

The BMR is the rate at which your body ticks over, and covers the number of calories your body needs to maintain normal functions, including staying upright (postural muscle action), keeping warm and all the other body processes. It represents the minimum level required to fuel the metabolism. The average Basal Metabolic Rate (BMR) is 10 calories for every pound (25 for every kg) of lean body mass. Lean body mass is the weight of your body excluding the weight of your fat. For example, if a woman weighing 120 pounds (54 kg) has a body fat percentage of 25 per cent (about average), that

means one-quarter of her weight is fat. A quarter
of 120 is 30, so she has 30 pounds (12 kg) of
actual body fat, leaving 90 pounds (40 kg) of lean
body mass.

Multiply this figure by 10 calories for every pound
(25 calories for every kilo) of lean body mass, and
that makes a total BMR of 900 calories per day. Now
work out your own BMR. First look back to where
you noted your body fat percentage (see page 40)
and work out what it is in pounds (or kilograms).
Subtract the answer from your total weight and
the result is your lean body mass. Multiply that
by 10 and you have your BMR. Note it down in
the box.

My BMR is:	calories
OMR Lean body mass XX lb × 10 = your personal OMR	Lean body mass XX kg × 25 = your personal OMR

• Step Two: Calculate your Physical Activity Requirement (PAR)

This refers to the energy used up in additional physical effort during the day, which increases the amount
of oxygen going through the metabolism. Just as a
fire burns more quickly with plenty of air, so does
your metabolism – thus increasing the amount of
fuel needed. Your PAR includes both formal exercise,
like jogging or an aerobics class, and other exertions
during the day, like running for the bus or digging

in the garden. It only refers to increased effort, not the sedentary basics of life like sitting at a desk, watching telly or sleeping, which are taken care of by the BMR.

Calculating an individual's Physical Activity Requirement (PAR) is difficult. At what point, for example, does mild exertion reach the point where it increases fuel needs over and above the BMR? The general view is that this is happening when an individual can actually feel their heart rate increasing – when you get breathless, hot and sweaty through exertion. Different physical activities make a range of increased calorie demands, depending how intense they are. Here is a table of physical activities together with their calorie expenditure.

ACTIVE CALORIE EXPENDITURE

Activity	Calories burnt per hour
Sports	
Aerobics	430
Circuit training	510
Running	400
Squash (competition level)	840
Swimming (competition level)	600
Swimming	400
Jogging	300
Cycling (competition level)	660

Hobbies	
Cycling (relaxed)	240
Walking briskly	360
Dancing	350
Disco dancing	400
Gardening (digging)	480
Gardening (general)	250
Housework	
Floor scrubbing	400
Ironing	200
Polishing	200
Vacuuming	250
Daily activities	
Climbing stairs	660
Strolling	240
Watching television	100
Sitting at computer	100

To work out your own PAR multiply the calorie consumption per hour for your activity by the number of hours per day on average that you perform it. For example, you might take your dogs for a brisk hour's walk every day (360 calories per hour), and you might also do an average (sometimes more, sometimes less) of 30 minutes circuit training (510 calories per hour) each day. That adds up to a PAR of 615 calories per day. Be very honest about exactly how active you are and fill in the box with your PAR.

My PAR is:	calories

• Step Three: Calculate your Specific Dynamic Effect (SDE) requirement

Specific Dynamic Effect (SDE) is energy expended by your body in response to food intake and is part of the process of digestion. Have you ever noticed that you get hot or flushed while eating, particularly when eating certain foods? What you are observing is the SDE in action. This stimulation of the digestive system increases your calorific expenditure requirement by about 10 per cent, which is one of the reasons why eating more can make you slimmer.

Miraculously, some foods – celery, lettuce, rhubarb, radishes, cabbage, carrots – require more calories to digest than they actually supply. So it is easy to see that you can increase your SDE by changing what you eat.

To calculate your personal SDE add together your BMR and your PAR and multiply by your body fat percentage. For example, say your BMR is 900 and your PAR is 700. Added together that makes 1,600 and multiplied by a body fat percentage of say 23 per cent, that makes a total of 368 calories per day. Now work out your own SDE and fill in the box.

My SDE is:	calories
BMR + PAR × %age of body fat =	

• Step Four: Add the elements to get your OMR

Now discover what your Overall Metabolic Rate is,

expressed in terms of the calorie energy you need to operate each day. Just add together the three figures in the boxes and you have the result. For example, a BMR of 900, plus PAR: 700, plus SDE: 368, would make an Overall Metabolic Rate of 1,968 calories in all – call it 2,000. Fill in your Overall Metabolic Rate in the box.

My OMR is: calories
$$BMR + PAR + SDE = OMR$$

The Metabolism Booster Plan

The Metabolism Booster Plan is going to work on every single component of your overall metabolic rate. The first element of the plan will feel like a miracle to someone who is a habitual dieter. It involves food, not just any old food but clever eating. We are going to make the science of nutrition work to our advantage. The Specific Dynamic Effect (SDE) will be boosted by eating more, and giving our digestion more work to do. Changing the way we eat – how often and what – will have an effect on the metabolism by enabling it to function more fully.

To burn efficiently the metabolic engine needs a good supply of oxygen – just like any other fire – so the second set of easy actions to take will be aimed at raising metabolic rate simply by increasing intake of air (oxygen).

The third area of trickery – discovering ways to increase physical activity – will have a two-fold effect. It will raise the PAR and also help build extra muscle, resulting in a greater lean body mass, which in turn increases the BMR.

> ## SHARRON DAVIES, Olympic swimmer, Gladiator 'Amazon'
>
> *'I'm not fanatical – it's little but often. I walk my dogs as often as possible. I drink too much cola and should drink more water, but I find it so boring.'*

The tricks used in the OMR are tried and tested by sportsmen and -women who use these techniques to help them perform physically at a constantly high level. Tom Deters, coach and health publisher, explains: 'Dieting for competitive sportsmen is more demanding than for the average person. Bodybuilders, for example, aren't just concerned about fat loss. Their goal is an alteration of body composition, which involves both the loss of body fat and the maximum development of muscle mass. This involves a lot more than just cutting calories.'

The average slimming cheat doesn't want to be a bodybuilder – but she can certainly identify with that goal of reducing fat and toning the muscles. So let's uncover the nitty-gritty of real, scientific nutrition with our first con-trick.

Fuel Burning Boosters

Nutritionist Steven Terrass is dismissive of many of the diet books fashionable today, saying: 'When you realise the complex processes taking place in metabolism it doesn't take a rocket scientist to understand that you must respect what is going on. It is nutrition that keeps it going, yet most people simply don't understand what is happening, and know little or nothing about nutrition.' As an example, Steven cites the complexities of just one aspect of the metabolism – the fuel in. Unlike petrol, human fuel – food – comes in many different forms, and we are going to use this to our advantage in our first cheat, eating differently.

Eating Differently

When I discovered this particular way of cheating at eating I was amazed. All those years of denying myself food were banished. No more spreading hated margarine on my toast. No more doing without delicious olive oil on my salad. It turned out that many of the things I had given up because of the calories could in fact have helped me slim, while the low-calorie substitutes weren't helping my metabolism at all.

STELLA TENNANT, model

Favourite meal: 'Carpaccio with olive oil, rocket and Parmesan. For pudding I'd definitely have a cocktail called a B52. Finn, my black dog, might have one, too.'

When I interviewed Steven Terrass over a huge plate of rich seafood risotto, the first thing he did was explode the dieter's myth that all calories are bad: 'A calorie is a calorie in one sense,' he said, 'but where the calorie comes from makes a big difference. Our diets provide protein calories, carbohydrate calories and fat calories – each of which ideally has a different function.'

Here are the main functions involving metabolism
which the three food groups contribute:

- **Protein** is converted into amino acids which are
  used to help power, build and repair the muscles.
- **Carbohydrates** are turned into simple sugars like
  glucose and fructose which are used to fuel brain
  activity and as basic fuel for muscle movement,
  keeping warm, and other body processes.
- **Fat** is used to create fatty acids which regu-
  late hormones and other body functions and
  help repair cell membranes as well as fuelling
  the heart.

Steven warns that these processes can easily be
disrupted if the metabolism is running below par –
perhaps because of dieting or poor nutrition. He gives
a three-point description of what should happen and
what can go wrong:

1 'As someone who wants to be slim I need my amino
  acids from **protein** to develop into lean muscle –
  but if I'm eating incorrectly or not taking enough
  exercise then they will actually develop into fat.
2 'I want sugars from **carbohydrates** to provide
  energy that is used up immediately, rather than
  being left over and converted into fat.
3 'I want my **fat** intake to be used for making hormones and prostaglandins and regulating body
  functions rather than being shunted into storage
  under the skin or around the abdominal cavity.'

Here's a check list of how our foods should be
metabolised if the OMR is allowed to work properly,
and what can go wrong if it isn't.

food group	fully metabolised result	poorly metabolised because of:	result
Protein 4 calories per gram	Builds and repairs muscle	Low oxygen, lack of correct amino acids	Excess fat
Carbohydrates 4 calories per gram	Provides correct amount of energy; fuels brain	Low oxygen, blood sugar problems	Energy left over stored as fat
Fat 9 calories per gram	Regulates hormones, fuels the heart, etc.	Processing, cooking	Excess fat

The result is grim in every case. To prevent excess fat it is important to look closely at each food group and discover ways to ensure it is metabolised as successfully as possible.

- **Eat more protein**

For humans, the best source of protein is meat. Because there has been so much publicity against animal fat recently, many dieters have stopped eating meat, without realising that it must be replaced with other sources of protein. The irony is that in seeking to reduce dietary fat (fat in food), they have also cut out something that will really help shift excess body fat (fat stores in our own bodies) – protein. Protein does this because it helps make a very important substance called L-carnitine. L-carnitine is a vital part of the process by which muscles burn energy, especially stores of excess body fat.

Think of a muscle as a furnace, and L-carnitine is the stoker who opens the furnace door and shovels in the fuel. And what is the fuel? About half of the fuel comes from fat stored in the body (sometimes more when you have been exercising for long periods). Stored body fat is held in cells called adipose cells, and what L-carnitine does is enable the fat reserve to be carried out of these cells and into the muscles where it is burnt for energy. If you don't digest enough protein to create sufficient amounts of L-carnitine, then the furnace door won't get opened. This causes several things to happen. The result that interests the slimming cheat especially is that the fat does not get into the muscles to be burnt, and therefore ends up staying in the tissues and the blood where you don't want it. Also, of course, it means the muscle furnaces burn less efficiently, leaving the individual feeling weak and generally lowering their metabolism.

Follow these protein metabolism boosters:

- Increasing protein can help you fight fat – you should also be especially careful to increase your protein if you feel tired or weak (both signs of protein deficiency).
- Vary your protein sources by eating fish, soya, beans and pulses, eggs, nuts, cheese as well as meat.
- Have your protein little and often – try a boiled egg for breakfast, a rich broth containing beans and pulses for lunch; or fish for dinner.
- For every protein portion (serving of meat, fish, bean curd, etc) eat roughly one portion of starchy food (bread, potato, pasta, etc), one or two portions of vegetables and one portion of fruit.
- Don't cut out meat just because you are worried about animal fat.
- Don't increase exercise without keeping up a good level of protein.

How much protein?
Conventional nutritional thinking recommends only 15 per cent of what you eat should be protein, but

recently this figure has been revised by a new theory that says we should eat more protein. An American nutritionist, Dr Barry Sears, who trains Olympic athletes and is the author of a controversial book called *The Zone*, suggests that we are eating too little protein and too much carbohydrate. He recommends eating 30 per cent protein, 40 per cent carbohydrates and 30 per cent fat.

The best quantity is probably somewhere between the two figures. Try this: approximately 25 per cent protein (more if you really do a lot of exercise), 50 per cent carbohydrate (this includes fruit and vegetables), and 25 per cent fat (including dairy produce).

Generally at least half of what you eat should be carbohydrates with the rest split between fats and protein, with slightly more protein than fat if you are very active and fit.

• Eat Different Carbohydrates

One of the easiest ways to cheat at slimming is to change the balance of the different carbohydrates you are eating. Carbohydrates are the big fuel source for humans, but they come in many different forms. For example, carrots and celery are carbohydrates, as are the 'starchy' foods like bread and potatoes. Foods as varied as sugar and bananas all fall under the carbohydrate 'umbrella', but their nutritional value varies according to which subgroup they are in (see below).

By switching the type of carbohydrate you eat, you can make a huge impact on your metabolism. Even something as simple as changing from white bread made from wheat flour to bread made from rye flour can help you become slimmer – without even needing to think about crispbread. Here is a brief guide to the four main carbohydrate groups:

1 **Refined Carbohydrate** This is manmade sugar obtained by refining it from complex carbohydrate sources such as sugar beet and sugar cane. It digests very rapidly to become glucose. A sub-group associated with Refined Carbohydrate is the Processed Carbohydrates – these are the highly processed manufactured 'junk' foods like biscuits, snacks and cakes where sugar (refined carbohydrate) is present along with other carbohydrates like flour (which is a complex carbohydrate, see below).

Change from refined to simple and complex carbohydrates:

2 **Simple carbohydrates** These naturally occurring sugars appear mainly in fruit. Fruit contains a simple carbohydrate called fructose, which is digested to supply the metabolism with glycogen, a type of sugar that is less liable to be laid down as fat.

3 **Complex carbohydrates** These are provided by starchy foods, mainly grains and the products derived from them, e.g., flour, bread and pasta; as well as beans and potatoes. These foods are digested to provide glucose, but some are more rapidly digested than others. The 'quick carbs' include white bread, wheat flour, potatoes and pasta. The 'slow carbs' include rye bread, rice and cellulose carbohydrates.

Include more 'slow carbs' and cellulose carbohydrates:

4 **Cellulose carbohydrates** These are provided by vegetables, in which the carbohydrate sugars are difficult to break down, usually within a mesh of indigestible cellulose (woody) fibres and water.

These cellulose and 'slow carbs' are a great ally for the slimming cheat because the glucose (sugar) they contain is much more difficult to digest than other forms of carbohydrate, which makes your metabolism work much harder. Glucose is the basic energy source required to fuel your metabolism; it is also used to make glycogen, to be stored in the muscles to power physical activity. As we know the ignition/digestion element of your metabolism uses up energy by the simple act of obtaining glucose from our everyday foodstuffs. If that glucose is difficult to obtain – as it is in the 'slow' and 'cellulose carbs' – then we don't get energy surpluses which, one way or another, always seem to end up as excess fat!

GOLDIE HAWN, actress

eats plain popcorn to keep hunger pangs at bay

The most easily available glucose is from refined sugar, while the most difficult to obtain is from cellulose carbohydrate. Carbohydrates break down to glucose at different rates, and the more you replace 'quick carbs' with 'slow carbs' the less likely your metabolism is to lay down excess fat. Here is a table to help you discern between the two:

QUICK CARBS	SLOW CARBS
milled wheat products	oat products
white bread	rye bread
sugar	fruit sugar
pasta	leafy vegetables
noodles	beans and pulses
white rice	brown rice
cakes	fruit

Some starchy carbs, like white wheat bread, break down into glucose quite quickly, and the technical term for this is having a 'high glycaemic index'. Eating too many of these 'quick carbohydrates' (including sugar) can result in too much glucose being released into the bloodstream.

In order to deal with this excess glucose the body produces insulin. Insulin is required to get excess glucose out of the bloodstream as quickly as possible, which it does by depositing it in the tissue cells, where it is stored as fat. When there is too much glucose flooding the bloodstream, there is a tendency for the body to produce too much insulin, which sets up a syndrome called 'reactive hypoglycaemia'.

There has been a great deal of publicity about this syndrome because it lies behind the so-called dieter's 'highs' and 'lows' – in which the amount of glucose circulating in the blood soars and crashes over the course of a day. When insulin and glucose are in balance, fat cells are able to release their energy stores back into the bloodstream to be taken away and used elsewhere if necessary (for example, during physical exercise or stress). But if reactive hypoglycaemia sets in there is too much insulin about for this to happen. Of course, this increases the chances of permanent fat being laid down. So anything which breaks the vicious circle is helpful to the slimming cheat, since it stops glucose being stored as fat in the first place, and it makes it less likely that the fat cells will hold on to it.

This means that switching from easily broken-down 'quick carbohydrates' to 'slow carbohydrates' has a double benefit: it makes the metabolism use more energy, and it helps prevent the insulin reaction.

One simple sugar is the slimming cheat's friend,

and that is the sugar that comes from fruit – fructose. This sugar is used quite differently by the metabolism. Excess fructose does not trigger the insulin reaction. Instead it is sent to the liver to be stored as glycogen where it helps to prevent hypoglycaemia.

Storing glycogen – in the liver from fructose, or in the muscles from slowly released glucose – is one of the best things you can do for your body; it does not encourage fat storage, it helps to prevent the insulin reaction, and it gives your muscles greater energy, which makes you more active. In turn, you use up more energy . . . all of which adds up to a virtuous circle that will get you slim without you even noticing.

Boost your metabolism by changing your carbs:

- Swap 'quick carbohydrates' for 'slow carbohydrates' (see table, page 116).
- Swap from wheat bread to rye bread (rye is much harder to break down than wheat).
- Eat more vegetables.
- Eat more fruit.
- Serve brown rice not white.
- Have porridge for breakfast – oats are a 'slow carbohydrate'.
- Other 'slow carbohydrates' are beans, pulses and vegetables.
- Reduce 'quick carbohydrates' like wheat flour, wheat bread, pasta, noodles and sugar.

- **Don't be afraid of fats**

After all the anti-fat publicity recently, most of us seem to live in fear of fat. The truth is, our bodies need fat to live, and the sort of fat we need most is also the most delicious. Natural, unrefined fats like butter, olive oil and sesame oil are used by the metabolism for a whole range of different functions. Artificial, over-processed fats – including many of the so-called low-fat dairy substitutes – are not of any real use to the body. Because the body is unable to use them, they are likely to be shunted into the body's storeroom as excess fat. So it is no more fattening and much more healthy to dip your bread in lashings of olive oil, or even butter, than it is to spread it with the latest dairy substitute.

Steven Terrass explains: 'Say you have a raw olive oil dressing on your salad. That is fat which will supply the metabolism with fatty acids that have a host of functions. The body can really get its money's worth from those calories. But if the oil has been hydrogenated to turn it into low-fat dressing or margarine, or it has been fried, it is chemically altered and the metabolism can no longer use it for this wide range of body functions. All it can do with it is to lay it down as stored energy – fat in other words.

'The end effect is as though you had eaten more of it than you have. Obviously if the metabolism isn't able to use the fat for its full intended range of functions then that leaves you with a lot of calories left over. Also, because your body can't do the manufacturing, it then doesn't run so well – therefore using fewer calories. So 20 calories of raw olive oil are not the same to the body as 20 calories of margarine. This is what the dieter should be thinking about.'

This is because fat – the so-called demon – is actually the most complicated and multi-functional of the three food groups. Fat contains the most calories of any food group – nine calories per gram, while protein and carbohydrate have only four calories per gram. This is one reason people have become so worried about it. But the answer is to make sure the

fat you eat is able to do its metabolic work properly.
Cutting down unnecessarily can be dangerous.

The heart, for example, derives its energy from fat
calories, which is why there were some cases of heart
failure during the 1980s' craze for very, very low-fat
diets. Fat is used by the body to make fatty acids,
which are vital partners in a huge range of different
metabolic processes:

- They can be used for manufacturing cell membranes and necessary compounds.
- They are extremely important in regulating hormones and prostaglandins. When women cut
  their fat intake too low, their hormonal system
  is disrupted, resulting in infertility – a common
  problem among athletes.
- Fats are also used for stored or immediate energy,
  but a slimming cheat obviously wants to reduce
  the storage element to a minimum.

Boost fat's work-rate:
- Do include fat in your diet.
- Get your fat from natural sources – dip bread in olive
  oil Italian-style rather than using margarine.
- Avoid chemically processed fats (e.g., butter substi-
  tutes, margarine).
- Avoid over-cooking fat which changes its biochemi-
  cal make-up as described above.

Changing Your Eating Patterns

Just changing the times you eat can speed up your
metabolism so that you can eat the same or even
more than usual without gaining fat. In a nutshell,

the best way to do this is to **eat early and eat
often**.

What a lovely piece of advice to be given! From a
metabolic point of view it also makes good sense.
The body's digestive enzymes and internal chemistry
are at their most active first thing in the morning,
so calories taken at this time will be used to the
maximum. So breakfast should be a substantial
meal, if possible. Boosting metabolic rates at this
time of the day by eating can help them to remain
high throughout the day – discouraging the body's
natural tendency to slow down in the afternoon.
Eating your biggest meal late in the evening is not
a good idea – this is when enzyme output is at its
lowest.

As well as helping to stimulate the metabolism, it is
possible to prevent the highs and lows of blood sugar
(reactive hypoglycaemia, see page 117) by eating little
and often. Eating a large rich meal sends a surge of
sugar into your blood. This not only leaves an excess
to be stored as fat but also triggers the insulin
response. One of the side-effects of too much insulin
is that it prevents a substance called Hormone Sensitive Lipase (HSL) from working properly. As the job of
HSL is to enable fat to be released from fat cells, this
means that not only are you storing extra fat, but you
are also failing to excrete previously stored fat. Fre-
quent small meals prevent the insulin rush and so
enable substances like HSL to function efficiently.

Use Super-Nutrition

Super-nutrition is the newest and most exciting of
the slimming tricks, and it is one that will rev up your

metabolism all on its own – even if you don't bother with any of the other cheats in this section. In order to function, the metabolism needs a whole range of vitamins, minerals and trace elements. The group term for these vitamins and minerals (which include trace elements) is 'micro-nutrients'. If the body doesn't get enough of these micro-nutrients the metabolism doesn't work properly and all sorts of illnesses can occur. If the body gets just about enough, near satisfactory, the metabolism functions well enough to avoid serious health problems. Nutritionists believe that the average diet provides this near satisfactory level of micro-nutrients. But if the body gets all the micro-nutrients it needs in plentiful supply, then the metabolism can function at its optimum level – meaning it can use up all its fuel to provide high energy, a strong immune system and a sense of well-being. From the slimming cheat's point of view it is the intensive use of fuel which is the most exciting aspect of this theory. In order to get this high level of fat-fighting micro-nutrients we need to use super-nutrition.

- Super-nutrition will help fight fat by boosting your metabolism and increasing your fuel use.
- The recommended way to get super-nutrition quickly is by taking supplements of certain vitamins and minerals.

Many nutritionists now believe that average eating habits do not supply enough micro-nutrients to achieve super-nutrition. They therefore recommend taking supplements. Here is a quick guide to the different supplements that are most involved in boosting the metabolism to reduce fat storage.

Key Metabolism Boosters

Use this guide to find out which micro-nutrients will help you raise your energy levels and decrease your body fat. It doesn't include all the vitamins and minerals that you need (vitamins A, D and E are among micro-nutrients omitted). Instead it concentrates on those micro-nutrients that are really important in triggering the processes that make your metabolism work. Those seriously interested in super-nutrition try to take their chosen nutrients as individual supplements so they can control exactly which and how much they have. Solgar make an excellent range of individual supplements, and they are available in good chemists and health food stores. Solgar also manufacture L-carnitine and amino acid supplements but these are fairly specialist products and you might have to find a sports nutrition supplier if you want to try them (e.g., the shop at your local gym or any body-builders' supplier).

If you are confused about which supplement to take, or just want a good all round boost, then choose one of the many multi-vitamin and mineral supplements available. Read the label carefully and make sure that it contains zinc, Vitamin B6, magnesium, Vitamin C, potassium and chromium – these are the key micro-nutrients from a slimming cheat's point of view. If it doesn't have them all, buy the missing ingredient separately. However, make sure it doesn't also repeat some of the other micro-nutrients because this might cause you to take in too much of a certain micro-nutrient.

Stick to the dose advised in the table below. The micro-nutrients listed here are safe, even at levels higher than those advised here, so you need not worry about over-dosing by mistake. However, any-body planning to take large – so called mega-doses – of any micro-nutrient should take advice from a doctor or nutritionist. Some vitamins, not those listed here, do have risks associated with over-dose. Vitamin A supplement should not be taken by pregnant women.

Micro-nutrient	Functions	Notes	Usual Supplement Amount
Zinc present in: meat, eggs, mushrooms, yeast	Involved in more than 200 metabolic functions, including growth, mood control, gland function, nervous system	Deficiency likely in dieters and can take a long time to build back up to optimum levels	10–30mg
Chromium present in: yeast, egg, wheatgerm	Involved in the insulin cycle to make Glucose Tolerance Factor (GTF) which helps regulate blood-sugar levels	Deficiency associated with food cravings; helps increase lean body mass	25-100mcg
Magnesium present in: soya, nuts, figs	Important in energy production, works in cell structure and repair	Often deficient in women, giving rise to PMS symptoms	200–500 mg
Potassium present in: yeast, fruit, vegetables	Stabilises body fluid levels, activates metabolic enzymes	Often deficient in women giving rise to distended abdomen, fluid retention	approx. 2g
Vitamin B6 present in: yeast, fish, wheatgerm	Vital component of metabolic processes, mood regulator. Needed to work with L-carnitine	Works with zinc to prevent depression	25–200 mg
Vitamin C present in: fruit, vegetables	Involved in most body maintenance processes. Needed to work with L-carnitine	Minor deficiency gives rise to chronic tired-ness, lethargy, muscle weakness	500mg

| L-carnitine constructed from protein | Crucial metabolic role in enabling energy to be used by the muscles | Once classified as a B vitamin, but closer to an amino acid. Supplement used to increase muscle metabolism | 1–3g |
| Amino acids | Derived from protein, used in the process of burning fat energy | Individual amino-acid supplements are used by body builders and as fat burners | variable |

Note: g = gram; mg = milligram (one thousandth of a gram); mcg = microgram (one thousandth of a milligram).

How does Super-Nutrition Work?

We all know that vitamins and minerals are important for our health, but it is only recently that bio-chemists have begun to discover just how vital and wide-ranging their functions are to the body's metabolism. Steven Terrass explains: 'In order for our metabolism to be able to burn food properly it requires a whole range of micro-nutrients which work together on the process of metabolising proteins, carbohydrates and fats.'

DENISE LEWIS, Olympic heptathlete:

'I'm working on strength and endurance and I'm trying to improve my speed and lose some weight. For nibbles I eat fruit, chicken sandwiches, bananas and raisins. I take multivitamins and vitamins C, E and beta carotene.'

Marked deficiencies of these micro-nutrient vitamins and minerals can have dramatic effects. Diseases like scurvy, rickets, pellagra and beriberi are all caused by lack of micro-nutrients. These diseases have now largely disappeared in the developed world due to our understanding of nutrition. Governments in the West now establish Recommended Daily Allowances (RDAs) of the most important vitamins and minerals, which has meant that government regulations for the vitamin enrichment of manufactured foods (for example of bread, flour and breakfast cereals) have been used to decrease these diseases in the West. But are those RDAs set at the right level? Certainly they are high enough to prevent the acute deficiency diseases, but are they high enough to ensure that the metabolism is working at its best?

This is the question scientists are now asking. Leading nutritionist Ann Walker has written: 'Nutritional science is entering a new era in which the recommended daily intake of key micro-nutrients is being based on optimal levels for health, instead of merely preventing deficiency symptoms.' When RDAs were originally laid down they were designed to set a minimum level, below which there was a genuine danger of an acute deficiency disease. RDAs were established at a time when nutritional science was in its infancy, and several vitamins had not even been discovered!

Scientists now believe that in order for the metabolism to function efficiently it needs much higher levels of vitamins and minerals than are currently recommended. And the bad news is that the latest research indicates that it is unlikely that many of us are getting those higher levels of micro-nutrients from our daily diet. Lorraine Perrett of the Institute for Optimum Nutrition points out: 'In theory our diet ought to supply sufficient micro-nutrients but the reality is that these days supplements are almost always essential.'

Chronic dieting puts you at an even greater risk of suffering from low levels of micro-nutrients. Ursula Arens of the British Nutrition Foundation explains: 'The less you eat, the harder it is to get all the nutrients you need.' So yet again there is an example of the vicious circle of over-dieting: by eating less we reduce our intake of vitamins and minerals, which means that the metabolism cannot work effectively, which lowers the OMR (Overall Metabolic Rate, see page 100), which means we need even less food energy and find it difficult to lose weight.

This process can set in very early on. Vitamin C, for example, is lost very rapidly from the body and deficiencies can occur in as little as a fortnight.

Steven Terrass says: 'You need high levels of the full range of vitamins and minerals to ensure that you fully metabolise the fats, proteins and carbohydrates that you eat. If this doesn't take place completely you will have an excess of them – which gives obesity and poor health. It will bring your body down. The more of these micro-nutrients you take in, up to the optimum level, the more efficient will be your metabolism.'

By increasing intake of micro-nutrients to a higher-than-average level, the slimming cheat can kick start her metabolism. Even better, there is increasing evidence to suggest that doing this may have the additional effect of combating modern-day diseases like heart disease and cancer. Ann Walker believes that new higher recommended intakes will be aimed at preventing degenerative disease and giving protection against the effects of environmental pollutants.

> **VERONICA WEBB, model, TV presenter**
>
> *'I take 2,000 milligrams (2g) of Vitamin C every day to give me energy and stop me overeating.'*

Steven Terrass goes even further with his controversial view that we will discover in the next decade that cancer and heart disease are in fact deficiency diseases themselves, just like scurvy and pellagra. He believes that they have not been discovered because they are slow to develop and set in at different deficiency levels.

He also warns: 'Many ordinary diets don't even go over the conventional view of deficiency level. Everybody requires some supplementation, but with dieters it is especially important, particularly if they are making a fresh start.'

One of the main symptoms of having micronutrient deficiencies is fatigue, so if you are one of those people who is 'tired all the time', or who falls prey to every single virus that goes round, or you find it hard to recover from injuries and other health setbacks, then super-nutrition is a must. And as a slimming cheat, it is one of the best tricks in your book.

Ignition/ Digestion Boosting

Burn more calories by actually eating more

By now it will be fairly obvious that you should not have to eat less to lose weight. Even if you already eat a lot, you need to *change* what you eat rather than eat less. Many determined long-term dieters actually need to eat more – though few of them realise it. The less a dieter eats, the less the SDE (see page 107) element of her metabolism is stimulated, reducing still further her body's calorie requirements.

The process of digestion alone uses up a lot of the calories that are being digested – even before other energy requirements are met. For example, about 23 per cent of the calories in carbohydrates are burned up by the process of creating energy stores – that is even more marked in those 'slow' carbohydrates we discussed earlier in the chapter. The more you eat, the more you can kick the SDE into action.

SANDRA BULLOCK, actress

allows herself Kentucky Fried Chicken as a food craving treat.

Eat more 'negative calorie' foods

Miraculously, some foods – including celery, lettuce, rhubarb, radishes, cabbage and carrots – require more calories to digest than they actually supply. Because the metabolism uses up so much energy in processing these foods, they could almost be called 'negative calories'. The main source of 'negative calories' are those cellulose carbohydrates we discussed earlier in the chapter. When you want to nibble or eat something filling, try these foods:

- raw carrots;
- coleslaw of raw cabbage, grated carrot and apple with orange juice and yoghurt dressing;

- celery stewed in stock or celery soup;
- raw cabbage with a yoghurt dip;
- raw brussels sprouts eaten whole;
- stewed rhubarb with honey and yoghurt;
- salad of lettuce, radish and tomato with olive oil;
- steamed cabbage with butter and pepper;
- vegetable soups of celery, lettuce, carrots, etc.;
- ratatouille of stewed vegetables;

BRYAN ADAMS, pop singer

is a vegan and follows food-combining principles. He has not cancelled a show in three years of touring.

Use your over-fat to help you get slimmer

Even being fat uses up energy! We may think of our fat cells as unwanted, lazy cells loafing around on our thighs, but fat cells are metabolically active, too. If stimulated properly they can not only take in fat but excrete it as well, thereby playing a useful role in the body as a legitimate energy store that can be called upon in times of need – such as hunger, pregnancy or during physical exertion.

Dieting, of course, attempts to simulate these times of need by producing an artificial famine situation. But the fat cells can only respond if they are in a metabolically active state. If someone goes on a diet who is a big eater, and probably still gaining weight though already over-fat, their fat cells will still be active. The fat cells will respond to the time of need, and fairly large amounts of fat can be shifted quite rapidly (if temporarily). This is what is going on behind the scenes of those 'I lost 10 stone' stories in magazines. The individuals involved almost always meet the various criteria for having active fat cells if:

- they are big eaters;
- they are very over-fat;
- they have never seriously dieted before;
- they have consistently been increasing their over-fat.

If this group of people, having lost most of their excess fat, then switch to being slimming cheaters, they will be able to maintain their weight and fat loss.

Another group of people who succeed through dieting also have metabolically active fat cells, though for different reasons. These are people who are normally slim but gain fat suddenly for some reason – through, for example, illness, medication, change of lifestyle, pregnancy or hormonal change. If these people diet, their fat cells will be active enough to let go of the excess. If the original cause of the sudden gain has been addressed, then they will remain slim and not need to diet again.

The vast majority of failing dieters have reached the stage where the metabolism is almost totally shut down. The fat cells are scarcely active at all. With so little food energy coming into them, they are not being stimulated to take in stores – and neither is there any trigger for them to let go of anything. Even if the body recognised a genuine need, it is doubtful whether there would be sufficient micro-nutrients available to enable the fat cells to be opened.

Under these circumstances eating more will actually stimulate the metabolism into renewed activity.

It is particularly helpful to get plenty of carbohydrates; nutritionists say: 'Fat burns in the flame
of carbohydrates'.

SOPHIA LOREN, actress

'Plenty of pasta made me what I am.'

Air Intake Boosting

Breathing Better

Slimming by breathing better is a simple and easy
long-term trick, yet very few people are aware of
it. The body's metabolism can be accelerated by
breathing more fully, and therefore allowing more
oxygen to enter the bloodstream. As any car buff
knows, one of the classic symptoms of too little air
entering a car's ignition is unburnt fuel dripping out
of the exhaust pipe. Much the same happens with the
body's internal combustion engine. If there isn't an
adequate supply of air, fuel is not burned completely
– but unfortunately for us the body's unburned fuel
ends up being laid down in fat cells. On the other
hand, if air intake increases, the metabolic engine
burns faster, using up more fuel energy.

This is one of the main reasons why aerobic (literally 'with air') exercise uses up so much energy and
is so calorie-intensive. Any form of exercise which
causes panting or heavy breathing is aerobic, and
has the effect of increasing the volume of oxygen
taken into the body. According to scientists there is a
direct relationship between this heavy breathing and

the amount of energy used up by the body. Just as a fire burns more quickly in a draught, so do the body's fuel stores.

So breathing more accelerates the metabolism, yet many of us do not breathe well enough for it to run even at normal level, let alone faster. It is not simply a matter of breathing in deeply that can provide adequate oxygen levels. The expelled breath is just as important, for it removes carbon dioxide and acts as a vital 'exhaust' system for the body. If breathing is incomplete, neither process is efficient. Statistics show that most people in developed countries use only 50 per cent of their breathing capacity.

Human lungs are deep, with a large volume. Ideally, oxygen should expand the whole of the lung when we breathe. The process of taking in oxygen and exhaling carbon dioxide should cause at least two-thirds of the air content of the lung to be exchanged every time we breathe in and out. But most people only skim the surface when they breathe, exchanging perhaps only the upper third of the lung's contents.

This shallow, incomplete breathing leaves much of the lung volume more or less stagnant. This can result in hyper-ventilation (over-breathing), persistent fatigue, poor concentration, interrupted sleep, and, of course, reduced energy requirement leading indirectly to over-fatness. The way to overcome all these problems is by discovering how to breathe properly.

It is common to describe something instinctive as being 'as natural as breathing', but, in fact, good breathing in many cases has to be learnt. One of the first areas that must be mastered by professional performers such as actors, singers and public speakers is controlled breathing. Athletes, too, discover how to exchange the maximum amount of air in their lungs in order to improve their performance.

For the rest of us, breathing is something we never really think about. The good news is that we can easily increase our energy needs without having to bother with special aerobic exercises, just by improving our breathing in day-to-day life. Ultimately, breathing better all day every day is much more effective than doing even the toughest exercise class once in a while. It is logical, and another great slimming trick.

Improving Posture

The most common cause of poor breathing is poor posture. In many cases, correcting long-term bad habits of posture – like hunched shoulders or slack tummy muscles – can radically improve breathing.

Christine Hocking is a professional instructor in Pilates, a remedial technique which improves health by teaching correct alignment of the body. She says, 'Poor breathing and poor posture go together. What you notice is that the poor posture creates a vicious circle of tensions in some areas and flabbinesses in others. For example, you would find someone with very tight muscles across the front of their chest which prevent them from opening out their shoulders and taking a deep breath in. This is often combined with weak, little used muscles round the ribcage, which means that they are unable to contract the muscles properly to push used air back out fully.' She goes on to describe the two most common forms of bad posture which create a series of breathing and figure problems.

• Kyphosis 'hunched shoulders'

This posture fault occurs in the upper back and shoulders, although it affects posture throughout the entire body. With this problem the points of the shoulders hunch round and down into the chest, leaving the shoulderblades sticking out, the chest muscles tight and the whole upper thorax closed and constricted. Christine comments, 'It is the classic posture of today's office worker. Go into any big company and you will see people sitting hunched over their computer keyboards in exactly this shape. This is what makes working on computer terminals so very bad for posture. You really should not sit still at your terminal for longer than 20 minutes, and you should get up and move around as often as possible.'

As well as constricting breathing, kyphosis also brings the head and neck forward and the chin down. That means that in order to lift the eyeline (to be able to see!) the chin has to be tilted upwards, causing the muscles in the back of the neck to contract. Tension in the neck muscles and shoulder muscles is a major cause of headaches, dizziness, fatigue and migraine. Check your posture now. Are your shoulderblades lying flat along your back, or are they thrust out like 'chicken wings'? Try to get your elbows to meet behind your back. Do you feel tightness across the chest and at the points of your shoulders? Do you frequently suffer from a stiff neck and tension headaches? These are all signs of poor posture which can restrict your ability to breathe properly.

• Lordosis 'pot belly/ swayback'

Although it can appear on its own, this form of bad posture is often linked with kyphosis. The rounding of the upper back puts pressure on the lower back.

This causes compression of the lumber curve which in turn pushes the abdomen out. As the abdomen protrudes it allows the digestive organs within to drop forward. This posture problem is often the cause of a protruding tummy, not fatness.

Most people's reaction to this is to try to pull in the tummy, but unfortunately doing this alone without correcting the basic posture problem just compresses the organs and creates digestive problems.

Christine explains: 'Women with bulgy tummies and sticking-out bottoms usually blame themselves for being fat, when in fact what is happening is that this lordotic curving is causing the pelvis (hip girdle) to sit on the legs slightly wrong. This is technically known as the anterior tilt of pelvis. The hip bone rolls forward and the bottom sticks out so you get that swayback, pot belly and the organs are slightly displaced.'

Do you suffer from a pot belly even though you are fairly slim elsewhere? Do you get lower back pain? Does your bottom bulge out when you are wearing trousers? Do you suffer from bloating and trapped wind? All these are symptoms of lordosis.

Pilates for Posture

Apart from affecting breathing, these posture problems give rise to specific figure problems. The next section of this book concentrates on all these individual 'body parts from hell' and there are particular exercises using Pilates style exercises and stretching to address each one. But to begin with, getting started on improving your posture will ensure that you are breathing correctly and getting the most oxygen in.

Christine Hocking has some tips for general overall posture improvement which will allow your chest to open up and improve the flow of oxygen.

1 Open your chest by allowing your shoulderblades to slide smoothly towards each other across your back and then pulling them downwards slightly. Use the muscles in your back to do this rather than forcing with your neck and shoulders.

2 As your shoulders settle into the right position you will feel your neck naturally moving back slightly, allowing your head to come into a direct balance over the top of the spine.

3 Settle comfortably in this position with your chin and eyes parallel with the ground.

4 Press your feet into the floor, and imagine you are pressing your head to the ceiling. See yourself as a taller person. Imagine you have pockets of air between the vertebrae.

5 Walk with your toes facing forward, chest open and weight of the head directly over the spine.

6 When carrying bags, keep your arms in line with your body, and carry them evenly on both shoulders.

Breathing Exercise

Christine Hocking stresses that it is important to get yourself into a good posture before you start this exercise to improve your breathing. Unless you are maintaining a good posture it will be impossible to move the muscles enough to do the exercise. She says: 'Many people will find correct breathing quite exacting at first, because they often have very weak intercostal muscles – the ones that move the ribcage to pump the lungs.'

For the basic 'Pilates' breathing exercise you need a long towel, exercise band or dressing gown cord.

1 Sit on the edge of a chair with your knees hip width apart and feet flat on the ground.
2 Fold your towel into a long, narrow shape and pass it round your back just below bust level as though you are about to dry your back.
3 Cross the ends over at the front and hold either end so that the towel is firmly wrapped round your ribcage just below your bustline, and hold tight with your hands.
4 Now try to take an ordinary breath in and out. If you are breathing properly you should find that you are unable to do this because the towel is preventing your ribs from moving. Those who breathe shallowly, without using their ribcage, will not find their breathing inhibited.
5 Now take another deeper breath in. This time as you breathe in, let the towel move to accommodate your rib movement. Be conscious of your ribs flaring upwards and outwards to make space for the maximum amount of air to come into your lungs. Be aware of how much the towel has to give to allow for this expansion.
6 When you breathe out, don't let the air come rushing out of your lungs. Try to use your muscles to push it out properly from the bottom as if squeezing toothpaste out of a tube.
7 Notice how much looser the towel is when you have finished breathing out.

Once you have practised this technique using the towel, put it into action in your day-to-day life.

This chest expansion is vital to good breathing – but slimming cheats might be interested to know that it is also fundamental to the illusionist's trick of escapology. Famous escapologists like Houdini used to expand their whole torso like this while they were being tied up, and once out of sight, collapsed their ribcage, allowing the ropes to slip off. So you really are a slimming cheat in more ways than one!

Benefits of improved posture

This simple trick of using breathing and posture gets results for the slimming cheat in many different ways. The most obvious is by improving the metabolism to achieve fat loss, and Christine Hocking confirms: 'We certainly notice this in my Pilates classes, there has been a lot of fat loss among my clients.' But she also adds, 'There are effects throughout the system – benefits to digestion, better health, less fatigue and a general sense of greater well-being and self-esteem.'

Like many of the non-diet answers to getting slim in this book, learning the art of good breathing has a doubled effect. Not only does it help shift excess fat, but it also leaves you feeling more dynamic – and thus more able to be energetic to use up even more calories. Feeling generally more lively forms the last of the metabolism-raising tricks – increasing your PAR level by getting physical.

Increasing Exercise

Even if you don't formally increase your physical exercise level in any way, you have already raised your activity level by improving your posture. Good posture is what the physiologists call 'dynamic', maintaining that it is an activity in itself and works on your muscle tone even while you are getting on with your life. So the slimming cheat has no need to enrol in yet another stressful and sweaty aerobics class in order to get physical.

At this stage you need to be conscious of your breathing and posture as much as possible as you go through your daily life. At first you will probably only be conscious of it at certain times – for example, if you are going for a walk at the weekend – but gradually you will be able to bring it into more and more of your normal daily activities. Try thinking about it when you are walking up stairs. Switching from lifts to using the stairs, and climbing with correct posture and breathing, can increase your calorie requirement as much as 10 times while you are doing it.

BRITT EKLAND, model and actress

cycles to the shops every day.

Your body only requires about 10 calories while standing in a lift for a few minutes but climbing up a couple of flights of stairs while breathing properly and carrying yourself well, and that figure will quickly soar to 100 calories or more. Try these easy activity increasers.

Dynamic actions

- When walking, do it actively, using good posture and full breathing. This will turn even a short stroll into an aerobic activity.
- While standing in a queue practise your posture. This uses up more energy than just slouching.

- Every time you look up at your computer screen or across the office, accompany the action by sliding back your shoulderblades to allow you to take a deep breath.
- Use the stairs not the lift.
- While watching television in the evening, sit properly in your chair and practise the breathing exercise (this will also help you digest your evening meal).
- Going round the supermarket, use the trolley as a prop to help you bring your body into a more upright position. This means you will be using your muscles more fully which has a slight 'weight training' effect.
- Although each individual effort may only take a couple of minutes, by the end of the day they can add up to a genuine increase in your daily activity level. This will have the effect of raising your overall metabolic rate.

The Cadbury Quotient

If you need something to motivate you in the quest to incorporate more activity into your daily life – whether formally or in the course of the day – it is useful to think of what I call the 'Cadbury Quotient'. This formula expresses any given exercise in the amount of minutes it would take to burn up 180 calories worth of energy, which is the number of calories in a Cadbury's Flake bar. The Cadbury Quotient table below makes revealing – and I hope motivating – reading.

THE CADBURY QUOTIENT TABLE

Activity	Approx. time required to burn 180 calories
Exercise activities	
stepping	18 minutes
circuit training	20 minutes
jogging	25 minutes
swimming (average ability level)	26 minutes
stationary cycling	31 minutes
weight training	37 minutes
Normal daily activities	
walking up stairs	25 minutes
walking (3 mph)	40 minutes
gardening	42 minutes
vacuuming	45 minutes
housework	50 minutes
ironing	60 minutes

Exercise physiologist and coach Paul Bromley explains: 'This element of increasing physicality in daily life is a holistic area. With this kind of activity, say, taking a brisk walk, a lot of things are happening at once which all work together to raise your overall metabolic level as well as improving general mood.'

He adds: 'Of course, the more we do this, the more muscle we build and that again will raise the metabolism because muscle is our metabolic engine; it is the only tissue that actually burns fat. The stronger it is the more active it is.'

Apart from raising the metabolic rate, strong lean muscles also improve the figure. To discover the secrets of body sculpting so that you can blitz your bad bits at the same time as enhancing your good features, move on to the next section.

CHAPTER FIVE

Self-assessment Questionnaire II
Where you should be cheating – target your
body parts

Cheat at Slimming may be about tricking other people into thinking you are thin or tall or glamorous or drop-dead gorgeous, but it is not about self-delusion. In order to wield your new arts of illusion to their best effect, you need to have a totally realistic perception of your body and your figure faults. And that is what this self-assessment and the following chapter are about. In order to do something about your shape and your figure, you have to face up to them. If you suck in your tummy every time you look in the mirror, and believe you have a flat stomach, you are going to face a constantly unpleasant (and uncomfortable) situation when your stomach fights back by bulging out through that tight little skirt. I will show you how to admit to yourself that you have a big tummy or other body part and then help you find ways to do something positive about it.

ANTHEA TURNER, TV presenter

'Before you start any course of self-improvement you have to look at your natural self and think, how can I realistically make the best of myself.'

Finally confronting the truth about your body can be a liberating experience. My own truce with my body dates from the day that I finally came to terms

with the fact that no matter how thin I got, nothing
would make me grow 3 inches (7.5 cm) taller. It was
then that I realised that my destiny was to be petite
rather than willowy, and I rapidly came to enjoy being
pocket-sized. Once you have understood what type
and shape of body you have, you can begin to make
the best of it. You can start to look better immediately
by dressing for what you are, rather than what
you would like to be. Fashion consultant Deborah
Shaw explains: 'Women don't understand their own
figures. It is important to make the conscious effort to
know yourself. A lot of women don't look too closely at
their body shape – and that leads to mistakes in dress
and styling. Whenever I am about to style someone
I start by asking them to look at the different body
shapes and define their own.'

There are two elements to this: body type and
figure shape. Body type is determined by genetics
and can be changed only very little. There are three
main body types: endomorphic (rounded), mesomorphic (muscular), and ectomorphic (rangy). One
of the great steps towards becoming a successful
slimming cheat is discovering which you are, accepting it, and then learning the tricks to bring out the
best in it.

All three types are attractive, with different good
points. Mesomorphs, for example, often look better
undressed than dressed – whereas ectomorphs are
the opposite.

In addition to the three main genetically inherited
body types, the fashion world recognises roughly six
different figure shapes. Certain figure shapes tend to
go with certain body types: endomorphs, for example,
tend to have pear-shaped figures while ectomorphs
most often have rectangular figures. Because figure
shapes tend to be determined by flesh rather than

skeleton, you can sometimes do something to change a figure shape (especially by exercise). There is also a lot you can do to disguise a particular figure flaw. The key to all these secrets will be revealed in the next chapter on how to 'Blitz your Bad Bits'.

First you must have a clear, realistic knowledge of your body type and associated figure flaws, so now is the time for self-assessment. Go through the questions and statements below, noting which are most accurate for you, and then look at the analysis to discover your body type and figure shape.

Body Type Assessment

1   Is your height
a   below average?
b   average?
c   above average?

2   Is your face shape
a   round?
b   square or heart-shape?
c   oval or oblong?

3   Are your feet and hands
a   small and podgy?
b   average size but broad?
c   long and narrow?

4   Are your limbs (arms and legs)
a   short and rounded in appearance?
b   average size, chunky looking?
c   long and slender?

5   Which of the following statements describes you most closely?
a   small and chubby.
b   stocky, muscular.
c   tall and willowy.

6   With which of these problems do you identify most?
a   I put on fat just by looking at food.
b   I find exercise more helpful than dieting but I always seem to look bulky.
c   Everyone calls me a beanpole but even when I exercise I don't seem to build muscle.

7   Whose figure is most like yours?
a   Dawn French or Roseanne Arnold.
b   Sally Gunnell or Mary Decker.
c   The Princess of Wales or Geena Davis.

8   When buying clothes, which is your biggest problem?
a   skirts too small, jackets too large when buying suits.
b   tops too small.
c   waist too tight, hips too baggy.

9   Which object would you compare yourself with?
a   pear
b   hourglass
c   banana

10   Is your best feature
a   your bust and shoulders?
b   your waist?
c   your legs?

Answers

Mostly 'A's – Endomorph (rounded)

If you scored mostly 'A's on the questionnaire, then your body type is that of a typical endomorph. You probably don't need telling that this body type could be summed up in one word: rounded. The classic endomorph has lots of round shapes in her body. Her face tends to be round and she usually has a thicker layer of sub-cutaneous fat (see page 30) which gives her arms, legs and torso a rounded appearance. Endomorphs are usually shorter than average, and their small (often round-looking) feet and hands are a tell-tale pointer to their body type.

Endomorphs are more prone to fat than other body types and have to work harder to stay slim than ectomorphs do. But if you are an endomorph, take comfort from the knowledge that in the West, you are not alone.

Laying down extra fat, and putting it on round the lower half of the body, is also a feminine trait, dictated by female hormones. So endomorphic qualities are really very natural and normal for women. Unfortunately, being the norm doesn't make it fashionable. Every endormorph is all too aware that hers is not the shape of the moment, while her exact opposite, the tall, slim, willowy ectomorph, is.

RUBY WAX, comedienne

'A beautiful woman couldn't do what I do. They simply wouldn't be able to handle the self-mockery. I mean, how many gorgeous stand-up comediennes can you think of?'

A century ago it was the other way round. Endomorphs represented great beauty; they were the models for artists in much the same way that photographers today want to snap only beanpole ectomorphs. In early Victorian times clothes were cut with round shoulders and full rounded skirts to accentuate a curvaceous, endomorphic look. So, short of waiting another 100 years for your body type to come back into fashion, what can you do to make your look closer to the current ideal?

First it is important to take on board the following considerations:

- In this country endomorphic is normal – it is the beanpoles who are unusual, not you;
- No amount of dieting is going to make you any taller or change the basic shape of your skeleton.

If you find it hard to come to terms with these ideas, or perhaps you dislike yourself in some way for being the shape you are, you will find a lot of help in Chapter Eight, which is all about the psychology of cheating at slimming. Those who are comfortable with the reality of their difficult body shape are already well on their way to becoming confirmed slimming con artists. The information contained in the next chapter will give you the tools you need to make the best of your body by zoning in on your bad bits and conjuring them away.

Endomorph figure shapes

The usual figure flaws associated with being endo-morphic are having a short waist or being pear-shaped. Pear-shaped people tend to have narrow shoulders, with their hips and thighs being their biggest body measurement. Very often they complain that they need a skirt that is one or more sizes bigger than their jacket. Sometimes in endomorphic people a pear-shape can be combined with a short waist. Whether or not it is part of a general pear-shape, a short waist is a figure fault that can be very difficult to diagnose. Many short-waisted women cannot understand why they still look or feel dumpy even when they have become very slim. It is yet another example of how getting thin is not the whole answer to looking good.

Short-waisted people tend to have a low bustline and a short distance between their bottom rib and their hip bone. This makes it difficult to find clothes that hang well, and a tell-tale sign is a waist band that rolls and folds over. Check out the appropriate blitz areas in the next chapter and you will find out all about how to combat and conceal your endomorphic figure problems.

Endo-ectomorph combinations

Occasionally a skeleton frame which is basically endomorphic – short-limbed, small-boned, under average height – is combined with the ectomorphic qualities of low body fat levels and little muscle. The result is what many people recognise as the 'elfin' build. One well-known example of this body-type is Kylie Minogue with her small, light skeleton and ultra-slim body. It is important to remember that this look is natural to only a few genuine endo-ectomorphs, and those endomorphs who attempt to emulate it run the risk of acquiring eating disorders.

Mostly 'B's – Mesomorph (muscular)

The mesomorph – literally 'middle shape' – body type is in fact less common than its name suggests. Its chief characteristic is muscularity, and since women are less muscular than men, the mesomorphic build tends to be more common among men. Mesomorphs are usually of average height, with a square or heart-shaped face. The key to a mesomorphic build is its strength. Not only does it give an appearance of strength, but it often is athletic and strong. The skeleton of a mesomorph tends to be broader, with stronger, thicker, individual bones than either the endomorph or the ectomorph. A classic giveaway of a big-boned, mesomorphic structure is thick wrists and broad hands and feet. If a mesomorph is fit, their bones are the frame for large, efficient muscles capable of explosive action like sprinting. If the mesomorph is unfit, she is prone to lay down fat instead of muscle. Either way the general appearance can look stocky.

This rather dense build is the down-side of being mesomorphic. Madonna made a typical mesomorphic transition from slightly plump and chunky at the beginning of her career to lean and muscular after she started working out – but she still isn't a willow, and never will be. The plus side of this is that the mesomorphic build is the most easily sculpted to create the body-shape you want. You can't change the shape of bones or fat, but you can alter the size, length and bulk of muscles. And since mesomorphs are more muscular their bodies respond well to the kind of body sculpting you'll discover in the next chapter.

True mesomorphs also find physical exercise easier

than the rest of us and therefore usually positively enjoy it, though endomorphs will find this hard to believe. So if you are mesomorphic it is time to stop bemoaning your stockiness and start to make your body type work for you. A bonus is that the two most common mesomorphic figure shapes (see below) are currently rather fashionable (indeed they are rarely out of favour with men).

Mesomorph figure shapes

Because of their musculature and good skeletal frame, mesomorphs tend to have rather well defined figure shapes, one of the more common being the hourglass. Hourglass-shaped women have what is sometimes regarded as perfect proportions: bust and hips with an equal measurement and a waist approximately 10 inches (25 cm) smaller. Surprisingly, those who possess this much-coveted shape can find it a problem when it comes to clothes.

Loose or untailored clothes don't follow the shape of the body and give the appearance of a much dumpier figure. Hourglass women find it hard to buy well-fitting trousers, and they have to be constantly on guard against unflattering, waistless fashions. Designers, especially in the 1940s and 1950s, dictated that the exaggerated inward and outward curve of the hourglass was what defined the ideal woman, but in the 1960s and 1970s an oblong or A-line was the preferred outline – to the despair of the curvy.

By the 1980s a different mesomorphic figure shape – the inverted triangle – was fashionable. Mesomorphs with their large bones tend to have broad shoulders, and if this is combined with a large bust, the rest of the body will appear to taper off by comparison. This look, which can be achieved with shoulder pads and uplift bras if not naturally endowed, was the epitome of the 1980s 'power woman'. In the long, lean 1990s it is less desirable.

Would-be mesomorphs

Despite the current fashion for rangy ectomorphs, the mesomorphic body type is probably the most commonly aspired to of the three types – simply because it is the one you can most easily pretend you are. Many an endomorph will claim to be strongly built, 'the beefy type', and fondly imagine that all that bulk is muscle rather than fat. It is the same with ectomorphs if they occasionally put on too much fat. There are a lot of mythomorphs around who are really endo or ectomorphs.

Mostly 'C's – Ectomorph (rangy)

If you have scored mostly 'C's, prepare to be an object of envy, because you have the current 'in' shape, that of the ectomorph. You are above average height, with long legs and slender arms. You actually find it hard to gain fat and stay naturally willowy most of the time . . . and we all hate you. Ectomorphs rapidly become used to this lack of sympathy from their non-ectomorph friends, but in fact there are downsides to this body type just as there are with the other two. Many ectomorphs would love to have curves; they hated being called beanpoles at school and long for a bust and a peach-shaped bottom.

Lack of strength and a difficulty in maintaining any sort of figure can also be a problem for ectomorphs. Throughout most of Northern Europe the ectomorphic build is quite rare for women, so many ectomorphs become self-conscious about the fact that they almost literally stick out at social gatherings. Many ectomorphs take up modelling. Hard as it is for non-ectomorphs to believe, ectomorphs can also have figure problems.

Ectomorph figure shapes

The most common ectomorph figure flaw is having a rectangular shape which basically does not have a waist. This means that there is nothing to define any other curves, so rectangular-shaped women tend to have very flat bottoms, no hips and probably a flat chest as well. Clothes hang extremely well on this shape, especially those cut on a long, lean line. But, when the clothes are removed, things don't look as good.

A classic example of this is the Princess of Wales, the envy of all, who surprisingly enough doesn't look quite so enviable when snapped on the beach in her bikini. Fashion editors know this phenomenon well and use a completely different group of models when photographing swimwear and lingerie. Another less common figure fault among ectomorphs is the apple shape, where fat has been laid down around the midriff. Although ectomorphs are not generally disposed to fat, poor eating habits and lack of exercise can result in over-fat, and this tends to go on in the abdominal area. See the Waist Disposal section (page 195) for details of what to do about it.

Ecto-mesomorph combinations

An unusual body type, especially among women, is that of the ecto-mesomorph, where someone has the height and long limbs of the ectomorph, combined with the strong bones and musculature of the meso-morph. In most cases the result is what is usually regarded as a physically perfect person; as you might imagine, many ecto-mesomorphs end up in sport or modelling.

Linford Christie is a good example of a male ecto-mesomorph with his broad shoulders, strong chest, muscular thighs and . . . we'll just leave it at that point I think. There are few female ecto-mesomorphs, but the Gladiator 'Nightshade', an Olympic athlete in her own right, is a perfect and, some might say, terrifying example.

Many over-fat ectomorphs fondly imagine them-selves to be ecto-mesomorphs, and you will often hear them explain that they are 'large-boned' or 'well-built'. In fact, when these people do succeed in losing fat they often turn out to be quite surprisingly narrow-framed and rangy underneath.

Body Types

	Endomorph	Mesomorph	Ectomorph
Key markers:	below average height	average height	tall
	short limbs	naturally muscular	long, slender limbs
	small feet and hands	even proportions	narrow hips
	small bones	large-boned frame	light-boned frame
	round face	square or heart-shaped face	oval or oblong face
Tendencies:	plumpness	can run to fat	usually thin
	short waist	large thighs	willowy-looking
	rounded appearance	stocky appearance	finds it hard to build muscle
	can occasionally be thin (e.g., Kylie Minogue)	finds physical activity easy – often sports people	can sometimes have high body fat
Figure types:	short-waisted	hourglass	straight
	pear-shaped	inverted triangle	banana-shaped
Celebrity examples:	Roseanne Arnold	Tessa Sanderson	Elle McPherson
	HRH The Queen Mother	The Duchess of York	Princess of Wales
	Dawn French	Sharron Davies	Laura Dern
	Ruby Wax	Sally Gunnell	Naomi Campbell

FIGURE TYPES CHECK LIST

short-waisted	low bust line; short distance between bottom rib and hip bones; waistbands tend to fold over
hourglass	same measurement chest and hip; waist approx. 10 inches smaller than chest and hip; same size jacket and skirt
straight	waist less than 8 inches smaller than bust or hip measurement; few visible curves; flat bottom
pear-shaped	narrow shoulders; hips and thighs biggest measurement; skirt one or more sizes bigger than jacket
inverted triangle	broad shoulders/large bust; narrow hips; jacket a size or more bigger than skirt
banana-shaped	waist measurement greater than hip/thigh; abdomen sticks out; long, slim legs

CHAPTER SIX

Blitz the Bad Bits

This is the section of *Cheat at Slimming* that is going to make a radical impact on the actual shape of your body. By now you have discovered how to wave that magic wand to give yourself an instant, superficially slim look; and you have learned the effortless long-term tricks that will leave you leaner for life. Now we get down to the nitty gritty, as we zero in on those specific body parts that it seems impossible to do anything about.

Nobody, not even the most super of models, has a completely perfect body. Everybody has a bad bit upon which we focus attention – particularly when we are feeling depressed.

MICHELLE PFEIFFER, actress

'If someone asked me who I most look like, I'd say Daffy Duck. I look in the mirror and say, "You are ugly, your eyes are puffy and you have big bags under them."'

The self-assessment on pages 147–60 will have allowed you to pinpoint your exact body type and the figure problems that go with it – whether it is big thighs, thick waist or an apple-shaped torso. Dieting has never been the answer to figure problems like these, because as everybody knows, you can't spot-reduce through dieting. Yet there are still diet books written which claim you can. This can actually emphasise a figure fault rather than cure it. Most British women will be familiar with the problem. You go on a diet and actually succeed in losing a bit of weight. The trouble is that it all seems to disappear from your top half, leaving your jodhpur thighs looking even larger and more out of proportion than ever.

If you've ever felt trapped by your figure fault, this chapter is going to be a revelation. Here is the first shock: it is possible to change the shape of your body. Unlike the other answers in this book, changing your body shape is neither instant nor easy, but it really can be done. The key to it is a combination of tough exercise and deep 'developmental' stretches which will physically sculpt your body into the shape you want. Physiologist Paul Bromley confirms: 'There is no doubt that exercise plays a part in changing people's body shape. By eradicating muscle imbalances and working on the strength and size of particular muscles you can produce the appearance you want.'

SHARRON DAVIES, Olympic swimmer, Gladiator 'Amazon'

'No one ever talks about stretching, which is really important in combination with cardio work and something you can do in front of the telly.'

Losing body fat at the same time enhances the effect, but it isn't totally necessary. Christine Hocking, a professional instructor in Pilates (see page 134), explains: 'People can look good and streamlined even if they are quite big or over-fat. It is all about improving your posture and body alignment to make you appear taller and slimmer – as well as having the side-effect of making you feel more confident and poised.'

The exercises and stretches to achieve this are undoubtedly tough – but they have a double effect. As well as changing the physical shape of your body, they will also increase your requirements for energy and so help you to burn up excess fat without noticing. Resistance training builds muscle, and muscle is active tissue that burns more calories than body fat, so the more muscle you have the more calories you burn.

US research shows that the optimum fat-burning exercise is a combination of aerobic and resistance work, which boosts lean body mass and metabolic rate. The routines described in this chapter concentrate on the resistance, body-sculpting exercises. If you add your own aerobic element by jogging, walking, skipping, swimming, exercise biking, or stair-climbing for even as little 10 minutes before you do your sculpting exercises, you will get results even faster. It is important also to use this kind of aerobic exercise so that you are fully mobile and warm before attempting the developmental stretches that are an important element of body sculpting.

LINDA EVANGELISTA, model

'You're born with what you have. But there are things you can do to improve yourself and exercise is one of them. You can change your body shape with exercise. You can colour your hair, put on make-up, get a haircut . . . there are things you can do. I don't believe in making yourself sick not eating because models in magazines are thin.'

Paul Bromley continues: 'Stretching contributes as

a secondary factor to the shape of the body. The stretch should come at the end of the work out and should be done in a controlled way, with individual stretches held for 20 seconds. This is very valuable in improving posture and correcting over-tightness in muscles.' He concludes: 'It is by reducing the body fat at the same time as increasing and shaping the muscle that you create the desirable, sculpted outline so many people are looking for.'

JODIE FOSTER, actress

Uses a routine of yoga poses and stretches to keep in shape

However, even an exercise devotee like Paul Bromley will admit that there are some elements of your shape that you can do little about. As we discovered in the self-assessment preparation for this chapter, there are three basic body types we are born with: endo-, meso- or ectomorph. These are determined by genetics which lay down what type of muscle-fibre you will have and what shape your skeleton is. Because you *can* improve your figure within your body-type, we have provided a series of optical illusions and artificial aids that you can use to cheat your way to the appearance of perfection when nature hasn't supplied you with the basics. If you want to be a total slimming cheat, you can also use these tricks on their own without bothering to exercise and you will get good superficial results. Best of all, though, is to use visual trickery to keep you motivated while you perfect the art of body sculpting.

Thigh Anxiety

Thick, heavy thighs can afflict endomorphs and mesomorphs, but almost never ectomorphs. They are most commonly associated with a pear-shaped figure, where the whole body is bigger below the waist. However mesomorphs with hourglass figures often complain of 'footballer's thighs', where the big quadriceps muscle is short and over-developed, giving chunky thighs even though they are not necessarily too fat. Heavy thighs may be combined with cellulite, which is a problem in itself and has its own section.

Along with the bottom, the thighs are the body part most often loathed by women – whether or not they are fat. Men usually find it very difficult to understand our permanent state of 'thigh tension' because they actually like women's thighs.

Human biology has provided a fat store on our thighs as a permanent emergency supply to keep women and, more importantly, their babies alive in hard times. Unfortunately, human biology has not changed to keep up with these feminist days when we are more preoccupied with getting into the boardroom than finding a safe cave, and dieting does very little to shift thigh fat. But we can cheat our way to better-looking thighs by using a combination of thigh-shaping exercises, and all the 20th-century tricks and illusions available to post-Stone Age woman.

Optical Illusions

The most important visual tactic for big thighs is getting the length right for dresses and skirts, and it is a trick that most of us get wrong. In the anxiety to reveal the slimmer bits of the leg, the common mistake is to choose a hemline that stops exactly where the fat part of the thigh begins. When the eye cannot see something it supplies an imaginary picture, based on an extension of what it can see. So if a hemline stops where the widest part of the thigh begins, the eye recognises the concealed part of the leg as also being thick.

If the hemline is dropped slightly so that it falls in the middle of the narrowest part of the leg, the eye assumes that the rest of the leg is equally narrow – and by magic you appear to have thinner legs.

This works in all the three main hemline areas – the thigh, the knee and the calf/ankle. If your thigh narrows just above the knee, as most people's do, then show your whole knee and in this way you can suggest that narrow above-knee portion continuing all the way up. If your thighs are big all the way down, then rest your hemline exactly in the middle of the knee – this is a flattering look for almost anyone.

Another good length is about 1 inch (2.5 cm) above the ankle bone – especially with high heels – as this focuses the eye on the narrow shapes made by the Achilles tendon.

Many women who dislike their thighs imagine they can never wear mini-skirts, but this is a myth. The correct shape of mini-skirt, teamed with the right hosiery, can do wonders for even the most thunderous thighs. The best shape of mini for large thighs is what I call the lampshade shape. It should rest loosely on or just above the hips and flare out in an A-line. And, if you dare, the shorter the better. The tulip-shaped skirt is a disaster because it follows the line of the bulge and then cuts into the thighs.

Deborah Shaw, manager of London's Harvey Nichols personal shopping department, advises: 'Put on your favourite shoes and tights, then use a towel to simulate the various different hem lengths by moving it up and down your body. Everybody – no matter what their thighs are like – has three different good hemlines on the upper leg, the knee and the lower leg. Once you get to know where they are, stick to them at all costs.'

Trousers are, of course, the biggest boon for the heavy-thighed, and even more so when flares and kick-back shapes are in fashion.

- Trousers enable you to lengthen the appearance of your leg by concealing high heels underneath. Even if you don't like high heels you can find a pair of shoes with slightly thick soles and stacked heels. Team these with a slight flare or 'boot-leg' to balance the width of your upper leg.
- Cruise-cut trousers which widen gradually right from the hipbones downwards are a clever way of smoothing the overall profile into a steady, straight line rather than a bulging one.
- Trousers with some form of detail on the outside seam (extra stitching, braid or a stripe) can take inches off the appearance of the thighs, because the eye stops where the block colour stops and the detail starts.
- The same tip applies to tights where a line of rib or a motif down the outside can work wonders.

Other visual tricks include creating a chevron –

downward-pointing arrow – shape which draws the eye upwards, thus lengthening the thigh. This is easy to achieve with a swimsuit by choosing high-cut legs, but you can also do it with dresses and skirts.

- Look out for dresses with an Elizabethan-style bodice which comes down in a V-shape.
- Choose tailored skirts and trousers with heavy seaming details echoing this chevron shape.

Avoid
- Tight, shiny leggings;
- tulip-shape skirts;
- mid-thigh hemlines;
- clinging materials;
- light coloured hosiery.

Artificial Aids and Cheats

• Learn to Love Lycra
The quickest, simplest and naughtiest cure for thigh anxiety is to take out shares in a multi-national company called Du Pont – the inventors of Lycra. Lycra technology is now so advanced that you can take your pick of hosiery products which will shore up your flab, gloss over your cellulite and generally make you the toast of 'thigh society' without ever having to move a muscle.

Forget those old-fashioned support tights that made your legs look hewn from the solid tweed; modern cosmetic hosiery is as sheer as you like. Wolford (whose Body Control range contains 24 per cent Lycra) and Donna Karan both have good selections which are available from department stores.

Look out for phrases like 'control top', 'contour' and 'shaper' to give you an idea of what the product is designed to do. Some brands have longer thigh control areas double-knitted into them and these are excellent for wearing under evening dresses as they give a very smooth uninterrupted line.

• **Pick Your Potion**

If your heavy thighs are combined with cellulite then it is worth using one of the creams discussed in the cellulite section on page 183. Keeping the skin in good condition will help to smooth the profile of the thighs, but no cream can actually make your legs thinner. For that you will have to turn to the exercises below. Remember though, that you can always resort to fake tan to reduce the whiteness and shine of your thighs, which will give the illusion that they are thinner.

• **Cosmetic surgery**

The surgical method of reducing the fatness of thighs is by liposuction. Early liposuction techniques were rather basic and consisted largely of vacuuming up the fat cells, causing considerable disruption to surrounding tissue. Modern methods are rather less invasive, but are still accompanied by considerable post-operative bruising, swelling, pain and some initial scarring. The operation is usually carried out under general anaesthetic – which is, in itself, a health risk. Leading cosmetic surgeon Dr John Celin recommends the operation for those who are young and healthy, and not generally over-fat. It is most effective for localised pads of fat – jodhpur thighs – rather than for cellulite. Performed correctly on the right subject it can be extremely successful, but if you are considering it, discuss it carefully with your family doctor and get a referral from him. Do not answer adverts; reputable surgeons do not advertise.

JODIE KYDD, supermodel

uses a foot soak in Aveda Miraculous Beauty Replenisher, which softens the feet and improves the circulation through the whole leg: 'Take care of the feet and the rest will take care of itself.'

Thigh Sculpting

For those with heavy thighs the good news is that the large, important muscles in the thighs respond better than almost any other body part to body-sculpting exercise. Sports physiologist Paul Bromley explains, 'Muscles are what dictate the outward appearance of your body, and if the muscle is a large one, like the quadriceps group in the thighs, then working that muscle will affect the person's body shape.' He makes the heartening promise, 'If you have a certain circumference of the thighs you can change it.'

The thigh-sculpting exercises described here should be done every day. You don't have to put on special clothes to do them, but make sure you have been moving around for a period of at least 10 minutes before you start – either as a formal warm-up or during daily activity. You will find these exercises tough and your muscles will be stiff at first, but they work.

Thigh Sculptor 1 – the Plié

Borrowed from ballet dancer's barre work, this exercise works especially hard on the outer thigh muscles to cure 'jodhpur' thighs.

1 Take your shoes off. Stand at right angles to a chair, desk, table top (or barre if you have access to one). Use one hand on the chairback to help you balance while you perform the exercise.

2 With feet hip-distance apart, turn your toes out as far as possible. Bend your knees until they are directly over your toes.

3 Tuck your buttocks in and raise your chest, looking straight forward.

4 Now raise your heels as far up as possible, going up on tiptoe with your knees still bent. Hold for a second before dropping your heels and repeating.

5 Do this as many times as you can – 20 times is a good number.

6 When it starts to hurt, stay up in tiptoe position as you move on to the next phase of the exercise.

7 In tiptoe position with knees out and bent, drop down about 3–6 inches (7.5–15 cm), and then back up again.

8 Remember to keep your bottom tucked in the whole way through the exercise.

9 Repeat this part of the exercise as many times as you can. If you can do 20 properly executed repetitions you are doing well.

Thigh Sculptor 2 – the Dip

Used by sprinters and weight-trainers, this is a truly evil exercise which gives dramatic results in shaping the backs of the thighs.

1 Stand with feet slightly apart about 2 feet (60 cm) in front of a step; the bottom of the stairs will do.

2 Stretch your right foot out behind you on to the step, so that the ball of your flexed foot is resting securely on the step.

3 Bend your left knee until it is directly over your left foot.
4 Now bend your right knee and drop vertically down until your right knee is nearly on the floor. Do not lean forward as you do this, come down in a straight vertical line – make sure your left knee never goes further forward than your left foot.
5 Straighten up again and repeat.
6 Perform the exercise 10 times on each leg. Don't be tempted to do more than this to start with. This is a deceptively tough exercise which will leave you feeling very sore if you overdo it. Build up gradually to 15 or 20 repetitions on each leg.

Thigh Sculptor 3 – the Stretch

Body sculpting is not just about working muscles; it is equally important to stretch the muscle in order to improve its shape. Many people with heavy, bulky thighs already have quite strong, firm thigh muscles but because the muscles are short and over-taut they give the appearance of width to the thigh. A programme of long, sustained stretches, known as 'developmental' stretches, helps these short, taut muscles to relax and lengthen.

Pilates teacher Christine Hocking says: 'Stretching will lengthen short bulky thigh muscles and give legs a longer, leaner appearance. These long, relaxed muscles are also more flexible. Over all, when the muscles are in good condition they give the body a much smoother, sleeker line.'

In order for a developmental stretch to work, your muscles must be warm and have a good supply of blood flowing to them. The best time is at the end of at least 10 minutes of aerobic activity. The ideal would be something like a brisk walk, followed by the first two sculpting exercises, then your stretches:

1 Lie on your back with knees bent, feet by the buttocks.

2 Lift your leg and gently grasp your right calf or ankle (whichever you can reach most easily). Straighten your leg until your knee is nearly but not quite locked.

3 Bring your leg towards your face until you feel a pulling sensation in the back of your thigh.

4 Breathing regularly and slowly, hold this position for a slow count of 20.

5 While holding the stretch, think of your muscle letting go and allowing you to pull your leg closer towards you. After about 10 or 15 seconds this may actually be possible.

6 At the end of the stretch, release very gradually and slowly return your foot to the starting position. Repeat on the other leg.

Now roll over on to your front ready to stretch out the front of your thigh:

1 Lying on your front, bend one leg back and reach out behind you to take the foot in your hand.

2 Bring your hand down and back, pulling your foot into your buttocks.

3 Keep your hips on the floor and think of the main stretch being through the front of your thigh.

4 After 10 seconds of stretch, lift your knee to increase the stretch, while continuing for another 10 seconds.

5 Come gradually back to starting position and repeat on other leg.

Developmental stretches like these don't work unless your muscles are warm and engaged enough to respond. If the muscle fibres are cold, then they will simply resist and tense even further. After developmental stretches, get up slowly and don't rush things for a minute or so in order to allow the muscle to become relaxed and springy again.

Cellulite Magic

Although it is not strictly a figure fault, cellulite is involved in so many different problem areas that it has a special section here. If you have cellulite, use the cheats and tips in this section, combined with those for the area at which your cellulite occurs.

Is Cellulite a myth?

There is a good case for saying that cellulite is just one more weapon in the battle between the sexes. Whether or not you believe cellulite is a myth seems to depend very largely on whether you are a man or a woman. For many years eminent male doctors and researchers have declared that cellulite does not exist. It is just fat, they say, there is nothing different about it: if you have excess body fat you will have it. For years this has caused women who suffer from cellulite to seethe with impotent rage. We know perfectly well that cellulite is a form of fat, but we also have the incontrovertible evidence of our own experience that it does behave differently from other forms of fat.

Its appearance – pouchy and lumpy – is different from smooth, flabby non-cellulite fat. It responds differently to diet and exercise. Where normal fat shrinks after a successful diet, cellulite often appears to get harder and more pocketed. Exercise too sometimes seems to exacerbate cellulite.

It now appears that cellulite is closely connected with female hormones. A new generation of doctors and scientists – mainly women – are now putting forward the view that cellulite does indeed exist, and that it does behave differently from other fat deposits.

So what is Cellulite?

Fat deposits which look lumpy and have a pouched, pocketed appearance, sometimes like the skin of an orange or sometimes with larger dimples, are peculiar to women. They appear most often on the thighs and bottom but also occur on the upper arms and knees. They are almost never found in any of the other common fat deposit areas of the body like the back or abdomen. It was French beauticians who first recognised that this kind of fat was different and gave it the name 'cellulite'.

During the latter part of the menstrual cycle, from ovulation onwards, the body has a tendency to store water and fat in order to prepare for possible pregnancy. During this time cellulite can become more marked, with the skin looking taut and bloated. This mild form of cellulite usually disappears at the end of the cycle. Long-term cellulite has the classic dimpled appearance. It can feel very hard and lumpy, and gives the impression that there are hard nodules of fat under the skin's outer layer. Some experts now think that this is exactly what is happening. They believe that cellulite is indeed tiny lumps of fat which are no longer part of the normal fat/fluid layer and its properly functioning cell structure. Overall, the current theory on cellulite is that it is fatty tissue that has been damaged through problems in the body's systems. The systems most likely to be to blame are the female hormones, the lymphatic system and the blood circulation.

Causes of Cellulite

Hormonal causes

Cellulite very often makes its first appearance at puberty, and it can become more marked after pregnancy and during Hormone Replacement Therapy (usually in the menopause). This tendency towards hormonal cellulite also appears to run in families, so some scientists are suggesting that there is a genetic factor involved in whether or not you will be prone. These elements certainly seem to dictate whether an individual will be more predisposed towards cellulite, but it is unlikely that the cellulite will become severe or stubborn unless other circumstances are also present.

Lymphatic causes

Many researchers are now convinced that a poorly functioning lymphatic system is one of the most important factors contributing to the occurrence of cellulite. The lymphatic system is one of the five main eliminative (drainage) systems in your body, along with the skin (excretes sweat), the lungs (breathing out carbon dioxide), the kidneys (expelling urine), and the bowels (excreting waste matter). It is the lymphatic system's job to deal with waste matter left

over from immunological (infection fighting) activity
and from body functions. The lymphatic system
forms part of the immune system.

These left-over products are mainly in the form
of waste-laden fluid in the tissue which must be
drained off and carried away by the lymph system.
The importance of this system is emphasised by the
fact that of the 50 litres of water in the average
person's body, a massive 40 litres is accounted for
by the lymphatic system with the other 10 being
devoted mainly to the blood circulation and the
digestive system. Yet the lymphatic system has no
power supply within the body to operate it. While
the blood's circulation is pumped by the heart, the
circulation of the lymphatic system relies on gravity
and the pumping effect of muscle contractions when
we move around; it also gets some help from the
blood system that runs parallel to it.

If the lymph system is not functioning efficiently,
waste-laden fluids remain in the tissues, which
gradually become saturated. Apart from the obvious
effect of visible fluid retention, this water-logging
results in disruption to cell structure and prevents
blood circulation and other metabolic processes from
occurring freely – resulting in metabolically inactive
tissue areas prone to cellulite.

Circulatory causes

It is thought to be the combination of poor lymphatic
drainage with low blood supply to the tissue which
results in fatty tissue thickening and hardening
to form cellulite pockets. It has been known for
some time that cellulite areas have very poor blood
circulation. The skin over areas of cellulite is often

cold to the touch, and women with cellulite often have associated problems like marbling of the legs and sensitivity to cold.

The lack of oxygen and other nutrients supplied to the cells by the blood leads them to become inactive and less able to expel toxic waste products. Fat held within the cells needs oxygen as part of the process which releases it back into the metabolism. Fatty tissue that has a good supply of blood will be easily accessed when the body calls for extra fat supplies to fuel energy needs. But fatty tissue in oxygen-depleted areas tends to shut down completely. The cell structure in these areas becomes rather like that of dead wood, with lots of thick, knotty fibres – and it is these that give cellulite its lumpy, pocketed appearance.

Lifestyle causes

Lymphatic and circulatory problems can occur for a number of reasons, due to lifestyle elements as well as genetic and hormonal causes. One major area which can be changed is a sedentary, inactive lifestyle. This contributes to cellulite in several ways. The lymphatic system, for example, is very dependent on movement in the major muscle groups. Someone who spends most of the day sitting will not be using the big muscles in the legs and arms enough to keep the lymph system pumping. In addition, sitting still on a chair for long periods of time has the effect of interfering with blood flow to the thighs and bottom and eventually damaging the tiny capillaries responsible for the micro-circulation of blood in that area. Poor posture can have similar effects in limiting the lymph and blood circulation by constricting the blood flow to certain areas of the body where the posture is cramped.

Another problem can arise with a poor diet, causing there to be a great deal of toxic metabolic waste to be disposed of – too much for the lymph to deal with completely. A diet including junk foods, highly processed foods, chocolate, etc., over a long period, allows the waste over-flow to build up. A short burst of unhealthy eating is not an issue, because the system can easily deal with this before returning to healthy function. Generally, any aspects of lifestyle which allow toxic build-up – like over-drinking, smoking or sugar-bingeing – can reduce the efficiency of lymphatic and blood circulation and give cellulite a chance to build up.

Cheat's Cures

For those with only mild cellulite, fighting the causes by improving lymphatic and blood circulation is usually all that is needed for a complete cure. But where cellulite has become well-established, the damage to the tissues is hard to mend, so in addition to treating the main problems, action has to be taken to deal with the effect. Curing cellulite has become an industry in itself, but few of the so-called solutions are really effective. Here is a cheat's guide to the clever answers which really do work.

Mesotherapy

Pioneered by French beauticians this treatment involves injecting medication directly into the cellulite-affected tissue by using a series of tiny needle

pricks. The medication injected varies according to
the therapist, but is usually a combination of various herbal preparations including artichoke and
chickweed. The main way in which mesotherapy
acts is by stimulating fluid drainage from water-
logged tissue. It is extremely effective and there
is a dramatic effect even after one treatment. A
course of 10 to 15 separate treatments is usually
recommended.

Mesotherapy effectively improves the appearance
of cellulite, banishing lumps and leaving a smooth
line. It is probably the most useful approach for
those with heavy or stubborn cellulite. But unless
the underlying causes are also treated, the cellulite
will return. So the best way of using mesotherapy is
as a kick-start to a longer term cellulite-banishing
programme.

Ionothermie

Another plant-based treatment of French origin,
ionothermie is a very enjoyable and relaxing treatment, quite apart from being effective in the short
term. A rich mud (sometimes a cream or gel), usually
containing extracts from algae and ivy, is spread over
the affected area. Next electrodes are attached and a
gentle electric current pulses through the mud, and
the skin surface with which it is in contact, as the
mud gradually hardens into a firm clay mask. The
passage of the current allows some of the active
ingredients of the clay to pass through the skin and
reach the underlying tissues.

This usually takes around half an hour, during
which time the client is kept warm, often in a dark-
ened room, and the whole sensation is very pleasant.

At the end of the session, the clay mixture is lifted off as a single cast. Most people experience a dramatic increase in circulation so that heavy legs feel light and there is a sensation of tingling energy – especially in thighs and bottom. The skin is immediately firmer, more taut and streamlined; many people lose inches off their thighs. The dramatic effects of the treatment wear off quite quickly so, combined with its energising effect, it is best as a pre-holiday or pre-party treatment. It is most suitable for those with fairly light cellulite.

An alternative treatment to ionothermie is the Celluzone Contour Wrap which you can use yourself at home. This contains ivy, butcher's broom and essential oils. All you have to do is smooth on the cream and then wrap yourself in the plastic film provided and then in a towel before relaxing for 30 minutes. This is an effective and pleasant treatment, but can be rather messy.

Treatment creams

Following the success of Dior Svelte Body Refining Gel, which has sold 10 million bottles world-wide in three years, there has been an explosion in beauty products claimed to reduce cellulite simply by smoothing a cream on the skin. Some of these creams really do work, but they use many different bio-chemical theories to try to achieve the same end result – less cellulite. Some of these theories are more plausible than others. To help you pick your way through this new minefield, here is a guide to the various ingredients used and the thinking behind them, together with a list of the more effective creams currently on the market.

Thigh Cream Contents

Ingredient	Function	Plausibility rating
Algae	improves lymphatic circulation	doubtful
Antioxidants	Vitamins A, C and E used topically to inhibit free radical activity and so preserve collagen elastin leading to firmer skin	very fashionable, but not fully proven as a topical application
AHAs (alpha-hydroxy acids)	smooth and help strengthen the skin surface	yes, proven in treatment of acne
Carnitine	makes fat burn faster	yes in test tube, but not proven to work externally
Essential oils	stimulate circulation and diuretic	yes, work through capillary micro-circulation
Plant extracts	horse chestnut for circulation, ivy for fluid retention and inflammation	possibly work like essential oils
Vitamin A palmitate	boosts collagen production	possible
Xanthines	caffeine derivatives including aminophylline, theophylline and kola – burn fat and curb storage	temporary effects, but more likely to be through diuretic qualities

A Consumer Guide to Thigh Cream Products

Product	Content	Effect
Annemarie Borline Cellulite Cream	tocopherol, caffeine, horsetail, rosemary	Heats up on application. Skin looks less spongy. Temporary.
Estee Lauder Thigh Zone	fruit acids and algae extract	Fills in the dimples by encouraging stronger skin growth. Improves skin condition, but not cellulite itself. Gradual.

Clarins Body Lift	plant extracts	Tingles, leaves skin tighter and smoother. Useful all-over.
Lancaster Recontour Anti-Cellulite Gel	Green coffee, magnetised micro-crystals	Aims to burn fat and improve circulation. Cooling effect on application, sensation of improved circulation. Immediate and lasting.
Dior Svelte Body Refining Gel	plant extracts	Market leader. Improves skin quality long-term, but not necessarily cellulite.
Boots No.7 Firming Anti-Cellulite Cream	theophylline, caffeine, carnitine, seaweed	Aims to metabolise fats

Many of the more successful anti-cellulite creams achieve their immediate, noticeable effects simply by improving the surface tone of the skin. Though they have not actually had an impact on the under-lying cellulite, they achieve a good superficial result by making the texture and structure of the over-lying skin more healthy. You can achieve the same effect yourself simply by taking good care of your skin. Keep it smooth and supple by using bath oils, moisturisers and massaging regularly – try some of the healthy detoxification tricks listed below.

Aromatherapy

Leading aromatherapist Robert Tisserand believes that essential oils are an excellent way of delivering active ingredients to the micro-circulation beneath the skin layer. He explains: 'The skin lets through a lot more than we used to think. An aromatherapy oil, which is partly oil soluble and partly water soluble, is particularly good because the oil aids penetration and prevents too much being lost through evaporation.'

KAREN PICKERING, Olympic swimmer

'I use aromatherapy for relaxation; I particularly enjoy an aromatherapy massage.'

A good anti-cellulite aromatherapy product is Elemis Aromaspa Cellutox Herbal Bath Synergy and Active Body Concentrate. This has a combination of algae extract along with juniper and lemon oils, applied first as a bath soak, and then used after the bath in the form of a cream. You can easily create your own anti-cellulite treatments using essential oils either in the bath or mixed with a massage oil and applied to the skin. Use a combination of two or three different oils with astringent, diuretic and soothing properties.

Aromatherapy oils for cellulite
Basil: promotes circulation
Cypress: detoxifying
Fennel: diuretic
Rosemary: astringent, stimulating, improves circulation
Juniper: freshens and tones
Sage: refines the skin surface
Lemon: stimulating, refreshing
Sandalwood: soothing, smooths skin surface
Geranium: improves overall skin tone
Cedar: detoxifying

NB. If you are pregnant or suffer from a health condition contact a reputable aromatherapist before using any oils.

Physical lymph stimulators

In addition to oils, there are various physical ways of stimulating the lymphatic system. Manual Lymph Drainage (MLD) is a gentle massage technique used to stimulate and free up the lymph system. Skin-brushing, as described on page 72, is also useful for cellulite. Do it with a dry brush on dry skin, fairly gently. Don't scrub.

Exercise is of obvious importance in encouraging the lymphatic system to function fully. Any exercise that uses the big, pumping muscles of the legs is good for lymphatic and blood circulation. Try to concentrate on movement that works the muscles slowly and rhythmically, like walking and swimming. These movements make the leg muscles contract regularly and evenly, improving blood and lymphatic circulation, pumping sluggish veins and lymphatics into action.

Regular flexing, stretching and extending the foot as in dancing also improves the return of lymph to the system. But try to avoid jerky, erratic movements, like sprinting, which can shorten the muscles. Short muscles tend to make cellulite look worse by keeping all the tissues in the leg bunched together, whereas long muscles have the effect of stretching the tissue and smoothing out the appearance of cellulite. Exercises that lengthen the muscle include swimming, walking, stretching and yoga.

The Bottom Line

Large bottoms are most often associated with pear-shaped endomorphs, but they can also afflict the

other two body-types. Banana-shaped women sometimes have lovely long, slender thighs which appear
to have been stuck on as an afterthought underneath
wide, square bottoms. Large bottoms have a number
of different causes. Some are not due to over-fat at all,
but are the product of bad posture which makes the
buttocks stick out unnaturally. Just improving the
posture has a dramatic effect on this figure problem.
Perhaps the most common bottom problem is the
spreading buttock which is due to a combination
of slack, under-exercised muscles and fat deposits.
This problem can be improved immensely without
the need for dieting, just through clever exercise.

But perhaps the biggest cause of what is perceived
to be a 'big' bottom is simply fashion. Women are
meant to be slightly pear-shaped; having a broad
pelvis is important for childbirth. Other cultures
with naturally small bottoms – like the Japanese
– buy padded knickers to emphasise their bottom
area. However, Western fashion currently favours
boyish, pre-pubescent bottoms.

Optical Illusions

According to Deborah Shaw, the most important
visual trick you can use to distract the eye from
a large bottom is to balance it against the body's
other proportions. She explains: 'Most of my clients
have a bigger bottom half than top half, because after
all, it is a fairly natural female shape. My answer is
to transform the outline from being a pear-shaped
into a perfect hourglass, and you do this by enhancing the bustline with the right tailoring and bra,
and by concealing small pads in the shoulders so

that the bottom is no longer the widest part of the silhouette.'

- The best skirts are those that drape softly rather than clinging to the figure – wrap-arounds in flowing fabrics are perfect for this.
- As with heavy thighs, the tulip-shaped or hobbled skirt should be avoided as it accentuates the bottom.
- Many women choose gathered skirts for comfort, but the big bunches of the gathers are not flattering. Instead, choose a box pleat which will tend to draw the eye inwards away from any bulges.
- Too tight a waistline can also have the effect of drawing attention to the bottom. Instead, create a longer line by wearing a straight, ribby sweater that ends just below the hips, or echo this shape with a tunic top.
- Shirt-style dresses give the option of moving the belt to your most flattering position.
- While trousers are a boon to big-thighed women, they can be a nightmare for those with broad bottoms. You are better off wearing men's jeans that are a size too large for you cinched in casually with a cowboy belt – this not only makes your bottom virtually disappear beneath all that denim, but also looks timelessly rebellious and hip.
- It is worth investing in a pair of well-cut dark cigar pants with the zip in the side or up the middle of the bottom. These trousers are a classic, which magically neaten the silhouette and can be dressed up or down for evening and day wear.

Using colour is vital for camouflaging the bottom – and few women understand the art. How often have you seen a large black-skirted bottom

to which the eye is irresistibly drawn by the contrast between it and the white shirt above and
pale tights below? Everybody forgets that black
can highlight just as easily as it can conceal.

- The best way to draw the eye away to better
  features is to make the bottom part of a gradual gradation of colour. It doesn't even matter
  whether it is darker or lighter than what is above,
  it just mustn't contrast.
- If you need to be formal try wearing a hip-length
  black jacket with a charcoal-grey skirt and neutral tights.
- Or for a more dynamic look team a ribby jumper
  in rust with a long claret-coloured wrap-around
  skirt and high heels.

Avoid
- shorts (at all costs!);
- highlighting your bottom in black or white;
- bulky, gathered skirts;
- tight waistbands.

Artificial Aids and Cheats

• Think Knickers

The visible panty line is the nightmare of the pos-
teriorially challenged. In order to overcome it you can
go two ways: either opting for a cover-up or simply
dispensing with the offending line. Modern thongs
are much more comfortable than the old 'G-strings'
used to be. The best designs have a full front and high
broad waistline which gives the added benefit of control and a smooth line over the stomach and waist.

- If your skin is firm and young then a thong is the best option. The tone of your own bottom – even if it is large – will give you a good line under clothes.
- If your bottom is flabby as well as big, then the large 'tap pant' style is a better choice. There are some wonderful new makes which include Lycra. One drawback of tap pants is that for those of us who are pear-shaped, a large bottom tends to be teamed with big thighs as well, so by wearing the pants the VPL just drops down to the top of the thighs where it can look even worse. But some new makes of knicker now have a longer leg which carries on the control right down to mid-thigh. These are wonderful in winter and give an excellent lean line.

• Cosmetic Surgery

Liposuction techniques can be used on the buttocks but most cosmetic surgeons agree it is better to lose the fat and tone the buttocks by other methods. If the buttocks then remain droopy there is a fairly simple operation which will remove the excess tissue and stretched skin and help bring back a tighter line to the bottom.

Bottom Sculpting

The buttocks are kept in shape by one of the largest muscles in the body – the *gluteus maximus* – and the way this muscle interacts with other muscles determines whether your bottom will be droopy, firm or sticking out. Christine Hocking explains: 'People are very surprised to discover that your stomach muscles actually have an impact on the shape of your bottom. The abdominals have to pull against the hamstrings and whether your bottom sticks out depends on how you work these muscle groups.' She explains that stretching and lengthening the muscles in this area is even more important than flexing and pumping them. So you no longer have to suffer the Jane Fonda burn in an effort to tone your bottom.

Christine says: 'A carefully performed deep stretch loosens hip flexors and stretches quadriceps, allowing the buttocks and back to come into a natural position.'

Bottom Sculptor 1 – the Lunge

Professional personal trainer Elliot Lancaster believes the traditional weight-lifter's lunge is the best overall buttock toner. Try it without any weights at first, but once you are practised, it is much more effective with a weight held in each hand or, if you have good balance, a bar (or broom pole) held over the shoulders.

1 Stand upright with feet hip-distance apart, toes pointing forward and knees relaxed. Hands by your sides.
2 Imagine your feet are the two base corners of a triangle, with the point of the triangle about 2 feet (60 cm) in front of you.
3 Lunge forward to put your right foot on to the point of the triangle, and bend the right knee so that it comes over your foot. The left foot stays where it is, but you will need to bend your left knee down nearly touching the floor in order to accommodate the lunge of your right leg.

4 Use your thigh and buttock muscles to push yourself back into your original standing position before repeating the movement with your left leg.

5 Keep up a steady rhythm, continuing until you have performed 10 repetitions on each leg.

6 Keep your head and eyes up and level throughout the exercise, and keep your upper body in balance over the movement all the time. Concentrate on using those thigh and bottom muscles very precisely and keeping your whole body in line rather than flopping about anyhow. This is what weight trainers call 'good form' and is very important to the exercise. The better the form, the quicker and more marked the results.

7 Aim to build up to 20 repetitions on each side. When even this becomes easy, add weights rather than increasing the number of repetitions.

Bottom Sculptor 2 – the Hip-Flexor Stretch

Attached deep in your pelvis, the hip-flexor muscles play a vital role in the alignment of the pelvic area – basically your bottom and hips. If these muscles are tight or in poor condition, the effect will be noticeable in the shape of figure flaws including a wobbly and big-looking bottom. The bottom is probably not actually any bigger, it is just that the muscles are allowing it to escape into the wrong place. This exercise works to increase the spring and elasticity of the hip-flexors. Because it is a stretch, do it when you are warm.

1 Lie on your back with feet close to the bottom, hip width apart.

2 Take your right ankle and place it on the middle

of your left thigh, so that your lower right leg is at right angles to your left thigh.

3 Press your right knee out slightly to give you room to create the stretch.

4 Now grasp the back of your left thigh in both hands (you will need to thread your right hand between your legs).

5 Gently pull your left knee in towards your chest. You may not be able to get very far before you feel a pull not only round your buttocks, but also inside your right groin.

6 Continue stretching, breathing slowly and deeply, for about 20 seconds while you try to increase the stretch. Repeat on the other side.

Bottom Sculptor 3 – the Deep Kneel

This deep, Pilates-style stretch teams very well with the hip-flexor stretch to help release your postural muscles and thus improve your figure shape. There are many ways of getting into the deep kneel; this one is a good, slow, gentle way of doing it. Have a cushion ready in addition to your mat for this exercise.

1 Kneel on the right knee, as if you are about to be knighted, and place the cushion under your right knee.

2 Now wriggle your left foot further out in front of you until you feel the stretch in the front of your right thigh.

3 Make sure your left knee is in good alignment over the top of your left foot.

4 Now reach round with your left hand and grasp your right ankle, bringing your right foot back and upwards as close as possible to your buttock.

5 You will find your shoulders come forward over
   your left knee and your lower back flexes. If
   you feel any pressure on your right knee, try to
   roll forward slightly more so that your weight is
   supported by the bottom of your right thigh.
6 At this point balance may be a problem. Until
   you are practised you can use your right hand
   on the floor to help support you. Once you are
   confident about balance, then stretch your right
   arm out directly in front of you.
7 Hold this pose for 20 seconds, concentrating on
   your form – your whole body in balance and
   alignment, your head and chin up and looking forward. To increase the stretch, dip your
   hips slightly down and forward and you will feel
   stretches through both legs, your buttocks, your
   back and your shoulders.
8 Repeat on the other side. When you have finished
   the stretch, gradually bring yourself down into a
   fully kneeling position before standing upright.
   This is a wonderful posture-enhancing pose that
   makes you feel great.

Waist Disposal

A fat-looking, bloated or protuberant abdomen or a
thickened waist seems to drive women to desperation
almost more than any other figure problem. This is
a shame because for most women, some degree of
curve in the lower stomach is inevitable, since it is
another of those sexual characteristics associated
with female hormones. In medieval days a protuberant belly was more highly prized than large breasts,

and the fashions of the day were draped so that women constantly looked slightly pregnant. Even today, psychiatrists believe a rounded tummy is still a subconscious turn-on for men, which makes it all the more baffling that the trend is to be as concave as possible below the navel. Fortunately, bulges in this area are more easily concealed than anywhere else.

ANNA FRIEL, actress

'Most men I know seem to like a woman to have a tummy. I think people get bored with somebody who is just placidly attractive, who just looks like a model.'

Apart from bulges, other midriff problems include short-waistedness. This can be a problem for endomorphic women who tend to have generally short proportions all round. Short-waistedness is a figure fault that can be hard to diagnose and is often mistaken for fatness, but once spotted it is easy to remedy. A less obvious midriff problem is for those lucky enough to have an hourglass figure. Superficially enviable, an hourglass figure can be quite hard to dress, if it is not to end up looking dumpy or overly buxom. The curves above and below the waist must be accommodated by good tailoring – which usually comes at a price – and the waist itself needs emphasis.

Optical Illusions

The easiest way to diagnose a short waist is by looking at the space between your hipbone and your bottom rib. You should be able to get at least a hand's breadth or more between the two – anything less is an indication of short-waistedness. Deborah Shaw recommends giving the illusion of length and line by using a belt to define the waist area. A belt slung loosely round the hips emphasises the difference between hips and waist. For those with an hourglass figure, a belt fitting snugly round the waist itself gives a neat outline and prevents all the curves running together. Deborah Shaw stresses: 'Hourglass figures should always define their waists, whether it is with tailoring in trousers or jacket, or with a belt, otherwise even a trim waist can look big. Big women with hourglass figures aren't exempt from this rule. They just have to be courageous – the result is that fantastic Marilyn Monroe look which men love so much.'

Fabric is especially important when it comes to camouflaging midriff flaws. Everybody has seen the nightmare of cheap, shiny fabric stretched into horizontal creases above and below a bulging tummy. The simplest way of avoiding this is by not wearing skirts that are too tight. I have often seen top women executives return from a business lunch half crippled by the fight between their swelling abdomens and their tight little power skirts.

- Choose firm, tailorable fabrics like gabardine and flannel which won't sag or stretch. A Lycra-weave fabric is also useful if it is heavyweight.
- The side zip which conceals a big bottom is also invaluable for tummies. Having a side zip in trousers enables the tailoring to allow a broad, flat central panel which has a flattening effect.

Probably the single biggest cause of the fashion for concave stomachs is the invention of the bikini.

- Tiny bikinis are just not user friendly to large
  stomachs, so opt for a full swimsuit or a bikini
  with a high-waist, tap-pant style bottom half,
  which is currently fashionable anyway.
- Above all, don't give up on your waist by moving
  waistbands above or below it – above and you will
  look pregnant, below gives the impression that
  you have 'builder's belly'.

Avoid
- tight skirts;
- micro-bikinis;
- bulky central zips;
- cheap, shiny fabrics.

Artificial Aids and Cheats

• Get Support
Until recently Lycra only extended its wonderful
support to legs and bottoms, but now it has moved
into lingerie as well as hosiery. The new Marks and
Spencer Waist-Sculpt knicker promises to reduce the
waist by an inch (3 cm), and there are plenty of other
brands which feature secret control panels dotted
about here and there to flatten your tummy and
whittle your waist. The Playtex Superlook Secrets
range includes micro-fibre to make it super-soft to
the touch. Warners Intimo collection (by Valentino)
has opted for the rather more old-fashioned approach
to waist-cinching by using boning and hooks and
eyes. The good news for the fashion conscious is
that old-fashioned corsetry is now very trendy, as
well as being a good figure-shaper.

• Think Thigh

Although designed to attack cellulite, those in the know apply thigh creams over the tops of the hips and stomach, where their skin refining effects can help smooth the line of the waist, though it won't reduce its size.

• Cosmetic Surgery

Abdominoplasty, the 'tummy tuck', is often considered by women desperate about their saggy, pot belly. However, cosmetic surgeon John Celin warns: 'Make no mistake, this is major surgery, performed in hospital under general anaesthetic and lasting up to five hours. Abdominoplasty patients stay in hospital three to five days while drainage tubes remain in the abdomen. During the next two weeks at home, you will not be able to stand up straight or sit down; sneezing, laughing and coughing will be uncomfortable.

'Abdominal supports and support tights will be essential for several weeks after surgery and you must watch your diet, or the fat apron could return.' So, apart from extreme cases, it's probably better just to dive straight into the Lycra without bothering with the intervening operation. For those with minor, localised fat pads, liposuction is an option.

• Desperate Measures

People predisposed to eating problems tend to over-react to a protruding belly or thickened waist. One recently fashionable tummy flattener is colonic irrigation. This method makes your lower abdomen flat by having the contents of your lower intestine 'flushed out' or irrigated. While it has certain medical applications for the chronically constipated or those suffering toxic conditions of the gut, this is not recommended on a regular basis since it makes the gut lazy and can leave it depleted in important intestinal flora (digestive bacteria).

Waist Sculpting

The waist is the area of the body perhaps most affected of all by the way we hold ourselves. The body has two main types of muscle. Big, strong 'dynamic' muscles, such as those in our buttocks and thighs, are used for physical activities and big movements. These muscles are easy to improve because they are designed for tough work-outs. The other main kind of muscles are called 'postural' and, as the name implies, their main role is to hold our body in position. They are in use nearly all the time as we stand, walk and sit at the desk but although they have stamina they are not good at large or active movements. These are the muscles that tend to get set into spasm and have tensions in all the wrong places if our posture is bad. Because the waist sits at just about our centre of gravity, it is the home of many of these postural muscles – and so this is where flaws in those muscles show up.

JANET JACKSON, pop singer

follows a vegetarian diet and undertakes a lot of stomach work to keep her waist narrow.

Bulges over the top of the hips and a short-waist can be cured fairly rapidly by re-aligning these postural muscles and improving the way we hold ourselves. Saggy, protruding stomachs respond much better to these techniques than they do to conventional sit-ups – so while everyone else toils at the gym, you can have a real impact by performing these gentle, specially designed exercises.

Christine Hocking explains: 'Exercises to emphasise good posture and body alignment strengthen weak muscles and stretch over-used ones, and this is much more effective than poorly performed exercises which just make posture faults even worse.'

Waist Sculptor 1 – the Back Extension

Elliot Lancaster says: 'Most people completely forget about the back half of the waist in their anxiety to work on the stomach, but weak or tense back muscles are just as much a factor in a saggy tummy and thick waist as the abdominal muscles themselves. If you only work on the front the abdominals can become over-tightened, resulting in a pot belly.'

1 Lie flat on your stomach with feet slightly apart.
2 Put your hands by your ears and use the lower back muscles to raise the upper half of your body off the floor.
3 Keep everything from waist downwards on the floor – don't let your feet and legs come up.
4 Gently roll back down again. Repeat 10 to 15 times. When you begin to find this easy, don't try to make it more difficult by straining to come up higher. The best way to make the exercise more difficult is by changing the position of your arms and hands. Experiment with this and you will find that the most difficult version is with your arms straight out in front of you.

Waist Sculptor 2 – the Latismus Slide

Most waist and tummy problems actually start in the upper back. When this area becomes hunched and rounded, everything underneath it sags. This exercise brings the upper back into alignment, resulting in a longer, smoother outline at the waist. Once you have become used to performing it on the floor, put the technique into practice throughout the day, whether you are sitting, standing or walking.

1 Lie face down on the floor with a small cushion supporting your upper chest.

2 Let yourself relax and you will notice that your shoulders drop down and your upper back is rounded.

3 Now you are going to flatten out your back by using the muscles in your mid-back, just above your waist, to pull first one and then the other shoulderblade back into alignment. The muscle group you will be using is called the *latismus dorsae* and it runs over the back and sides of your ribcage.

4 So, working first on the right side, slide your shoulderblade over your ribs, in towards your spine and slightly down towards your waist. Feel this as a very simple sliding motion controlled by the muscle below your shoulderblade. A common mistake is to perform the movement by tightening the muscle between the shoulderblades (the trapezius), which leads to tension and leaves the *latismus* weak and unused.

5 As you perform the movement you will notice how your whole shoulder moves up off the floor and your shoulderblade ends up lying absolutely flat across the back of your ribcage. Leave it there while you bring the other shoulderblade across to join it.

6 Now both shoulders are back and both arms are slightly off the floor. Using the same *latismus dorsae* muscles you used before, lift both arms very slightly higher. Only an inch or a couple of centimetres is plenty, but you must use only

the *latismus dorsae* muscles to achieve the movement. Don't use the arm muscles or the ones on
top of your shoulders or between your shoulderblades. If you don't find the exercise difficult you
aren't doing it properly.

7 Hold this for 10 seconds, gradually trying to build
up to 15 seconds. You will almost certainly find
your muscles shake. Release and repeat a couple
of times. Incorporate this movement into daily life
and try to allow your shoulders to remain comfortably in the new position – you will be amazed at the
difference it makes to the line of your midriff.

Waist Sculptor 3 – the Spinal Curl

This exercise aims to unlock the vertebrae of your
spine, particularly in the waist. By freeing up these
vertebrae it can actually achieve a physical lengthening of the spine – improving the outline of the waist
and even making you look taller.

1 Stand about 6 inches (15 cm) away from a wall
with legs hip-width apart. Let yourself go back
until your bottom and back are resting gently on
the wall.

2 Starting with your head, roll downwards until
your head is down by your knees and your back
is completely curled away from the wall, with only
the very bottom of your tailbone still resting on
the wall.

3 Now you are going to uncurl very slowly and
roll back up against the wall. Starting with the
vertebra immediately above your tailbone, move
it back to the wall and then continue to uncurl so
that you can feel each individual vertebra come to
rest against the wall one by one.

4 Almost nobody can do this exercise first time.
   Depending on where your stiffnesses are you will
   be able to get the sensation of each individual
   vertebra hitting the wall, one after the other,
   very clearly at some points, and not at all at
   others. Sometimes you will notice a whole section
   of spine – perhaps three vertebrae – hitting the
   wall at once.
5 Don't worry about this at first, just get yourself
   into a position with your whole spine flat against
   the wall as gradually as possible. Now curl down
   again, concentrating on taking each vertebra off
   the wall one at a time. It should be slightly easier
   going down because you have gravity to help.
6 Repeat the uncurl process and see if you can avoid
   the times when two or three vertebrae clump
   together.
7 Try to perform the exercise two or three times
   a day. As your spine mobilises and lengthens,
   incorporate the new posture into daily life for full
   waist-whittling effect.

Bosom Enemy

Given that most women wish to reduce every other
dimension of their body, it is surely illogical that
when it comes to breasts, bigger is generally regarded
as better. This is because the later 20th century has
made breasts the primary sexual focus. It wasn't
always the case. In between the wars, flappers actually used to bandage their breasts to make their
chests look flat, and breasts were no big deal in the
Middle Ages, either. At other times nipples, rather

than overall bust size, were what counted. The more daring of those supposedly demure, muslin-clad Jane Austen girls would have applied a little rouge so that the dashing Mr Darcy might just be able to discern them beneath a mist of Nottingham lace.

Despite these different fashions, it seems that what counts with men is having breasts at all. Current sociological research shows that even today, when pneumatic is supposedly ideal, equal numbers of men prefer small breasts. The ultimate message of this must surely be that we should all make the best of our breasts – whatever their size or shape.

Optical Illusions

A common figure problem as women get older is what Deborah Shaw calls the inverted triangle: 'This is where someone has a large bust which overpowers narrow hips and legs, looking very top heavy. It is really important to break up this overwhelming top half by having a V-line at the chest.'

She recommends a V-neck jacket, a shirt with the collar open, or a sweater with a V-neck.

- Other ways of creating this V-shape include wearing a long pendant or a long scarf with the knot resting just between the breasts.
- Fussy necklines or a lot of detailed pattern or stitching round the chest should be avoided.
- Old-fashioned yokes, gathers and pleats are also a bad idea as they create the 'bolster-breast' look which used to be so favoured by school mistresses.

- Halter necks and spaghetti straps on evening clothes and swimwear also need to be avoided, since they can give the impression of more flesh than there actually is.

  Small-breasted women, on the other hand, want to emphasise the bustline and they are lucky that this is easier than ever to do without the need to resort to silicone.

- The quick guide is simply to forget every styling rule in the book – go wild with shiny and tight stretchy materials, all of which give the illusion of curves.
- Padded and wired bras are an obvious choice, and one trick the celebrities use is to buy a cup size too small, in order to get that cornucopia spilling over look.
- A make-up artist's trick which is useful for evenings is to dust the cleft of what little cleavage you have with a little shiny bronzing powder, giving the impression of a deeper shadow than really exists.
- Don't forget that many breasts that appear small are actually just low and benefit immensely from exercise of the pectoral muscle.

Avoid
- bolster bosom;
- a low bustline, whether bosom is small or large;
- too-narrow straps on a large bosom.

Artificial Aids and Cheats

• Woman's Best Friend
The best and most obvious aid for busts is the bra,

yet what should be woman's best friend very often turns out to be her worst enemy. Fashion editors constantly complain to me that women will not get themselves fitted for bras. Most women just pick a bra that is the same as their jacket size, but your chest size and your bra size are two completely different things. Take a woman who knows her jacket size is 34 inches (85 cm). Unless she is totally flat-bosomed her bra size is going to be anything but 34. Her bra size will be the actual circumference of her ribcage (measured just underneath the breast), plus the bosom itself, measured in cup size.

So the 34-inch (85 cm) chested woman in fact has a bra size of 32 inches (80 cm) round the ribcage, and a B cup-size (the average cup size of the breast). For larger-breasted women this makes a huge difference.

Someone whose jacket size is 36 may still only have a 32-inch (80 cm) ribcage but be a C-cup or more. When this woman buys a size 36 bra the overall size will be too large to offer support, but the cup size will probably be too small, forcing the breast to overflow into the armpit.

The next time you buy a bra, ask the assistant to fit you and recommend the correct size. A well-fitted bra will give a whole new, lean line to the upper body, allowing the waist to become visible and smoothing the whole profile of the torso, as well as making clothes hang better.

Choosing the best bra for the job is also important now that there are so many different styles of bra on the market. Larger-breasted women should look at cross-over strap bras where the centre of gravity of the breast is in the middle of the back rather than under the shoulder blades as in a conventionally strapped bra.

• Breast Creams

Clarins has offered a range of breast products for many years, but this area of the beauty market is about to explode, following the success of contour creams for the lower body. The skin over the breasts and collarbones has a tendency to be thin, dry and sensitive. If you want to avoid the crocodile handbag look featured by the older generation of Hollywood celebrity, it is vital to take proper care of this area. Always protect it from the sun and keep it thoroughly moisturised.

• Cosmetic Surgery

John Celin describes us as 'a chest-conscious society' and since breasts are a primary sexual characteristic it is likely that to a greater or lesser extent we always will be. The first recorded breast enlargement operation was as long ago as 1895, and since then the whole question of breast implants (augmentation mammoplasty) has become fraught. Fortunately fashion is beginning to turn away from the ludicrous, and quite possibly dangerous, excesses of the 1980s.

The new cosmetic alternative to augmentation is a mastopexy or breast lift. This operation does not use any artificial implant to make the breast any larger, but instead lifts the breast back into a youthful higher position to give an improved figure outline. This is a much less invasive operation than breast enlargement, with few of its complications, and there is almost no visible scarring.

While breast enlargement has a bad reputation among the medical profession, the opposite operation, breast reduction, is regarded completely differently. For women with genuinely over-sized breasts, a reduction is regarded as a helpful and successful operation and can be obtained through the NHS.

However, breastfeeding is rarely possible after a reduction operation.

Body Sculpting

Whether it is too big or too small, or just plain saggy, there is no bustline which is not improved by good posture. Many women who dislike their large breasts attempt to conceal them by hunching their shoulders, but this just results in lowering the bustline so that it merges with the waist. The postural exercises in this section will help to cure this. Press-ups are the best exercise for raising the bustline by tightening the pectoral muscles.

Good 'form' is particularly important with press-ups. Most people think they know how to do a press-up, but unless the back and bottom are in a straight line and the body's weight properly distributed between the arms and the toes, press-ups will not be effective. If you have not done press-ups before, use the box position on hands and knees, but progress to the 'T-position' with legs straight as soon as possible. Your elbows should bend to right-angles and then straighten completely during the press-up – but it is not necessary for your nose to touch the floor. Start by repeating only five times, but build up to two sets of 10 repetitions as quickly as you can.

Arm Offensive

Arms never used to be a problem for many women because, as Grace Bradberry, style editor of *The*

Times, remarks, 'you just never saw them'. These days global warming and efficient central heating mean our arms are subject to as much over-exposure as any Los Angeles celebrity's. But arms are still neglected and forgotten until the moment of the swimsuit or evening dress, when mottled skin, folds of flesh, dimples, cellulite and wadges of fat suddenly become visible. Though our arms are not very notice-able to us, they are very obvious to other people. Just flick through any society magazine and one of the first things you will notice is all those bare arms – many of them completely spoiling an otherwise carefully perfected look.

Optical Illusions

For arms that are short as well as plump it is often a better option to reveal more rather than less. Choose halterneck tops which take the eye uninterruptedly from the neck, over the shoulders and down to the wrists, thus giving an illusion of length. Another way of doing the same trick is to wear tops with slightly too large or cut away arm holes, again including the shoulder in the arm length.

The length of sleeve has very much the same effect on the appearance of your arms as the hemline does on your legs, so when choosing sleeve length you should use the same principles.

- Opt for a sleeve that ends right on the narrowest part of your arm. Most people have three main narrow points: about 2 inches (5cm) above the wrist; about 1 inch (2.5 cm) above the elbow; and just above the bicep. The most flattering of all is the three-quarter-length, wrist-revealing sleeve, which gives length to round hands and emphasises the wrist bones, the least likely area to carry fat.

Avoid
- sleeves which end in the middle of the bicep;
- tight armholes;
- sleeves which end on the point of the shoulder.

Artificial Aids and Cheats

• Skin Creams

Thigh creams can be equally effective on the arms as on the legs. Keeping the skin of the arms in good condition makes an impact on the overall appearance. Most people forget about the arms even when they are meticulous about other body parts. Use skin brushing – especially on the elbows – and plenty of moisturiser. Remember, too, that fake tan creates exactly the same illusion blended on to the arms as it does on the legs.

• Cosmetic Surgery

Several different operations are available which can transform the appearance of saggy, bulging upper arms. The classic 'arm lift' (brachioplasty) is used to correct 'batwing arms' where – due to ageing or major fat loss – large folds of skin hang down off the upper arms. This operation removes the excess skin leaving a scar hidden on the inner side of the arm, and is usually very effective and successful.

Another version of this operation deals with the elbow and tightens the skin over the area. Smaller fat pockets in the arms can also be treated with liposuction. An alternative where skin tone over the elbows especially is a problem is the chemical 'peel' to renew the surface layer of the skin.

Body Sculpting

Like the thighs, the arms have large dynamic muscles – the biceps, the triceps and the deltoids – which are dramatically improved by training. The arms, though, need even more special attention than the legs because these days we use them very little. For example, there is now really no everyday activity that adequately exercises the triceps muscle at the back of the arms. So without specific extra exercise, the backs of the arms rapidly become fat and flabby as we age.

Arm Sculptor 1 – the Tricep Dip

Elliot Lancaster recommends two sets of 12 to 15 repetitions of this truly exhausting exercise.

1 Find a firm chair or bench approximately 18 inches (45 cm) off the ground and perch your bottom on it, with arms straight down either side of you and hands clasping the edge of the seat or bench.
2 Now walk your feet forward and slide your bottom off the seat so that your weight is being supported by your arms and hands.

3 Bend your elbows and dip your bottom down until your elbows are bent at right angles.

4 Now straighten your arms and bring your body back up again, using only the muscles at the back of your arms between elbow and shoulder – the triceps.

5 Repeat 10 to 15 times. The further away you move your feet, the less body weight they will support and the more difficult the exercise, to the point where your legs are straight out, resting on your heels, and the majority of your body weight is going through your arms.

Arm Sculptor 2 – the Lateral Raise

This works the muscle that goes over the top of the arms and shoulder (the deltoid) and gives that wonderful shaping and definition to the shoulders that we all crave when it comes to evening wear. You need a decent pair of dumbbell weights for this.

1 Stand upright with feet hip-width apart, knees relaxed and looking straight ahead. Hold the dumbbells next to each other in front of your stomach.

2 Raise both arms out to the sides until they are level with your shoulder, elbows straight but not locked, and knuckles facing the ceiling.

3 Hold for a second and then bring your arms back to the original position, being sure to control on the way back down as much as you did on the way up.

4 Repeat the exercise 10 to 15 times, remembering to puff your breath out as you raise the weights, and suck a new breath in on the way back down.

Arm Sculptor 3 – the Shoulder Stretch

The muscles in the arms are like those in the thighs – large and dynamic – which means that they can become bunched and over-taut. Again, stretching is the answer to encourage a desirable long, lean line.

1 Find the corner of a wall, or a door way or the edge of a bookcase or something similar, and stand about a foot away from it.
2 Raise your arm level with your shoulder and rest your palm flat against the wall corner, with your body facing the same way as your palm.
3 Now makes as if to walk away, but leave your hand in position. Move your feet as necessary until you feel a stretch through your upper arm and the top of your shoulder.
4 Increase the stretch by pressing your shoulder forwards. Hold for 20 seconds, breathing gently, before repeating on the other side.

Face-Saver

As a race the English do not generally have cheek-bones. Visit any Slav country and you will see bone structure you could build a house on. In Italy they have long, narrow noses and sexy almond eyes. But in England we have rosebud lips and plump, pink cheeks. All this is determined by bone, which cannot be altered by any amount of facial exercises or diets. Short of keeping your skin in good condition by not smoking, and following a thorough cleansing and moisturising routine, there is little you can do to change your face – except cheat.

BARBRA STREISAND, actress/director

*'I made it without getting a nose job. I learned
that I can be the best I can be and not be obsessed
with looks.'*

Optical Illusions

London hairdresser Michael Desport says: 'Apart
from make-up, the most dramatic impact you can
make on your face shape is in the way you have
your hair cut and styled. Depending on where the
stylist puts the hair, the eye can be drawn wherever
you want – but if the hair is in the wrong place it can
emphasise flaws. Few people realise that your face
shape is actually determined by the shape of your
whole head – a long narrow skull for example will
give an oval face shape. Your hairstyle should fit
your skull shape like a glove. If it is cut too small
the fit is not there and it makes the head look small.
If it sits away from the skull – as you often see with
"big hair" – then it overwhelms the facial features.'
Michael has provided these tips to discuss with your
hairdresser:

- To slim the face keep the hair away from the jaw
  and create width elsewhere in the style to balance
  the face.
- To create cheekbones, try a short haircut with
  detailing like feathering pointing into the cheek
- Try to emphasise strengths rather than just concealing weaknesses. If someone has nice eyes, for
  example, then concentrate on that area.

- Balance out the face to create symmetry.
- When you are trying to work out your face shape, leave your hair wet and comb it back, and don't look at the hair, look at the face. Bear in mind that your face can change over the years.

Artificial Aids and Cheats

• Make-Up

As someone who has worked on dozens of photographic sessions I know exactly the power of clever make-up when it comes to concealing facial flaws. There are super-models whose magazine-cover faces you may think you know as well as your own, but I can guarantee you would not give them a second glance without their hair and make-up professionally prepared. Make-up people are indeed artists, wielding light and shade to highlight bones and hollow out cheeks. They can narrow a nose, reduce a chin or strengthen a forehead. They can give you starry eyes, knife-edge cheekbones and rosebud lips. Theirs is such a complex art that I can give only a few pointers here. If you give yourself one slimming cheat treat this year it should be a professional make-over.

CINDY CRAWFORD, model

'A woman's face is her armour. If you wear the right amount of make-up, you can survive anything. I don't think many women realise how little it takes to look a lot better.'

• Shine

Shine catches the light and attracts the eye, so use it on the features you want to make more prominent.

Gloss and shine should be used with care. If you have a pad of fat under the eyebrow, avoid shiny eye-shadow as it will make it seem more prominent and distract from the eyes themselves.

• Shadow
Should be used for face shaping and outlining. Be careful with shadow because products which are dark in colour and seem to be shadow can in fact be shiny and light reflecting, thus highlighting areas you may have been trying to de-emphasise. Matte shadow is good for face-shaping: under the chin to conceal a double chin; round the jaw line to slim a plump face; down the sides of the nose to narrow it.

• Cheekbones
This is the most frequently incorrectly made-up feature. Emphasise cheekbones naturally by applying shine on the top of the bone itself rather than trying to hollow out the cheeks with a shadow powder. Be sure you know exactly where your cheekbones are – most of us judge them rather too low. Give a huge grin when applying shine and you will see your cheekbones to best advantage.

• Eyes
Top make-up artist Glauca Rossi stresses: 'The eyes are nothing without the eyebrows. Eyebrows are the picture frame for the face.' On a plump face you are better off strengthening your eyebrows and leaving your eyes with just a touch of mascara. Too much make-up on the eyes, particularly liner, can have the effect of closing them down and leaving them as specks in a large face.

• Lips
One of the first rules in make-up is never to emphasise both eyes and lips together. Strong eyes and lips

fight each other and make it difficult for the eye to rest on one feature. To counteract fat cheeks or poor cheekbones, match a strong mouth with eyebrows and less eye make-up, thus creating a balanced frame to compensate for weak bone structure.

• Spectacles and sunglasses

As every film star knows these are an absolute godsend. The right frames can give you a completely different face shape. Treat yourself to a new pair of sunglasses this summer, but buy them from a proper optician who can advise you on how to enhance your face shape.

• Face Creams

Not very long ago the question of whether potions and creams – face-lifts in a jar – worked or not was simply not worth asking. The answer was that they did not. Today, though, a cream which promises to brighten the skin surface or increase elasticity of the skin may very well achieve exactly that. The problem is to sort out those claims which are achievable from those which are not.

The first myth to break is that anything applied to the surface of the skin – topically – cannot possibly have anything but a superficial effect. In fact, much can be absorbed by the skin and transported into the bloodstream by the capillaries. This is how hormone patches work, and why other medications are increasingly being administered topically.

Another myth is that skin creams, despite their technical-sounding descriptions, do not contain genuinely active ingredients. Today many good-quality skin creams do contain ingredients which have a real biochemical effect. Very often though, the company producing the cream plays this down for fear that government regulations will term it a medicine, which means that the product must undergo much more stringent testing than for cosmetics. If anything, all this leaves the consumer even more bewildered than before.

Just when we had got used to the idea that it was all just cold cream, no matter how pricey, it appears that some products may really be worth the cost. But which ones?

Good ways of spotting genuinely active ingredients are looking at the shelflife and presentation of the product. Any product that has a sell-by date or must be kept in the fridge is likely to contain a genuinely active ingredient. Another clue is where one ingredient is kept separate from the other – say, in an ampoule or microscopic sphere or even a separate bottle – and the two are only mixed together just before application. Look out, too, for those products containing vitamins, which can be readily absorbed into the skin's micro-circulation. For this reason pregnant women should avoid any cream containing Vitamin A.

• Cosmetic Surgery

Nowadays there are so many different facial surgery operations available that it is possible to reconstruct your entire face. It is no longer necessary to suffer a bulbous nose, a receding chin or non-existent cheekbones. However, it is all the more important to be cautious before deciding to have facial surgery.

Some operations, like cheek and lip implants, have been rather discredited recently. There is a lesser-known operation that can have a dramatic impact on a face that continues to look chubby, long after puppy fat days. In many cases this effect is caused by fat pockets in the upper and lower eyelids, which tend to give the whole face a puffy look, even though anyone but an expert would be hard pressed to pinpoint why. An operation called 'blepharoplasty' removes these fat pockets and widens the eye, brightening the whole face and making the cheekbones more noticeable. The tiny white scar left by the operation is concealed in the upper and lower creases of the eye.

CHAPTER SEVEN

Self-assessment Questionnaire III
Your cheating heart – Are you thinking thin?

Not everyone who diets is over-fat; and not every non-dieter is slim. Grasping the significance of these statements is vital if you are to discover how to think thin. People who think thin are the people who remain naturally slim throughout their lives; they belong to that tiny and enviable portion of the population who do not diet and are not over-fat. The rest of us basically fall into three groups:

- we diet and we are over-fat;
- we diet and we are not over-fat;
- we do not diet (or rarely diet) and we are over-fat.

Whether or not we are in reality over-fat, the important thing that members of all these three groups has in common is that we do not have a slim person's outlook on life. This is apparent from the fact that we are either dieting or over-fat, or, in some cases, both. The other common factor, of course, is that without exception all of us in these groups long to have a slim person's outlook – to think thin – almost more than we want to be thin.

JASMIN DOTIWALA, presenter, The Word

'I eat anything. I don't eat really unhealthily but I will eat anything. I really don't believe in healthy food all the time – if I see a cream cake I'll eat it. The amount I work out and put my body through I feel I should be able to eat what the hell I want.'

On the journey to thinking thin, the first rule is to know yourself. The following questionnaire is going to help you to discover what dieting group you fall into, and how you have been failing to 'think thin'. Once you have gained a realistic understanding of these things, you will be introduced to all the different mind games you can use to get yourself slim the cheat's way – just by thinking yourself there.

Section One: Are you being honest with yourself?

For this self-assessment to work, you must face up to the facts about yourself and your dieting and how over-fat you really are. You may imagine that this is totally irrelevant to you, but research over the past two decades into obese (over-fat), satisfactory, and anorexic (chronic under-eaters) people has come up with some very interesting results about how honest people are with themselves about whether or not they are too fat.

Before researching this book I would have said that most people know deep down whether or not they are too fat without having to resort to the weighing scales or any other form of obesity measurement. In my experience, I usually know if I have let some extra fat creep onto my stomach or thighs, no matter how much I might suck in my tummy or try to find the best angle in front of the mirror. At first I might try to wish it away or make excuses, but eventually I have to face the fact that it's there. Having studied research into the psychology of obesity I have discovered that although this is the classic response pattern among people who maintain a stable, relatively satisfactory figure, it is far from normal for everyone. People who are chronic over- or under-eaters usually find it very difficult to perform accurate self-appraisal. In other words, with the best will in the world they find it almost impossible to be 'honest' with themselves.

A study took a group of obese people and a group of anorexic people and asked them to draw life-sized 'honest' outlines of their bodies. The obese people consistently under-estimated their bulk, while the anorexic people over-estimated their size. This difficulty in seeing ourselves as we really are is a real problem that is frequently overlooked. So how can you discover whether or not you are being honest with yourself? Go through the three different groups outlined below and you will be given tips about the games the mind plays. By the end of the assessment you will have a much more detailed and realistic knowledge of your psychological diet profile, and you can use this to put into practice the tricks described in the next chapter.

Section Two: What slimming psychology group do you belong to?

Group A Genuinely Over-Fat

Psychologists believe that many obese people remain consistently over-fat because they genuinely under-estimate the size of their bodies. They see themselves as smaller than they really are. If you suspect you are a body-image under-estimator there are lots of objective measures you can use which will overcome the problem. One trick is to start measuring yourself concretely against the rest of the world. For example, is your dress size bigger than the average? It's difficult to lie about that one – either you find it hard to go into a High Street store and buy clothes you can get into or you don't.

Sizes 14 (US size 10) and under make up 58 per cent of the female population of Britain – just over half of us. The flip side of this is the much vaunted statistic that 42 per cent of us are size 16 (US size 12) or over, and there has been much recent lobbying that there should be more clothes catering for this group in the shops. What the lobbyists conveniently forget, however, is that the statistics for this group coincide with the percentage of over-fat women in this country. So the chances are that if you are in that 42 per cent, you are likely to be over-fat. Now I hope it will be obvious from what you have read so far that this book doesn't regard this as a moral issue. Whether you want to reduce your over-fat or not is up to you. If you simply want to conceal it, this is the book for you. And if you want to do nothing about it at all, that's OK too! But whatever you decide to do, it's as well to start from an informed position.

In theory, a quick glance at a height/weight chart should be helpful in determining obesity but the knowledge that the charts don't tell the whole story often gives the under-estimator the chance to cheat herself. She tells herself she's bigger-boned, more muscular, a little bit taller than she really is – we've all done it. A good way of overcoming this natural tendency is to ask yourself whether you are bigger/plumper than nearly everyone you know, despite being much the same height. 'Yes' answers to these kinds of question should bring you face to face with the fact that you are indeed over-fat – whether or not you are the kind of person who likes to see herself only in a good light. Check out the categories below to see exactly what your slimming psychology is.

Over-fat categories

• Failing Dieter

According to the statistics, this is one of the most common of all of the slimming psychological profiles. As a Failing Dieter you have faced the fact that you are over-fat and dieted in an attempt to lose that over-fat. That diet, and probably many succeeding diets, has failed and you remain over-fat in spite of repeated diets. This category applies to roughly 40 per cent of all dieters. As you will have discovered already, the good news is that this book is written very much with you in mind. You should already have discovered many clever ways to break out of the failed diet trap, and in the next chapter you can find out about the ultimate cheat – the self-confidence trick.

• Chronic Obese

This category covers the group of people who have always been genuinely over-fat throughout their lives, yet have never attempted to lose that over-fat through dieting. These days this is a much smaller group than 30 or even 20 years ago, yet doctors estimate that perhaps 15 or even 20 per cent of over-fat people in Britain never go on a diet. If you are part of this group, this book is probably the first slimming book you have ever picked up. For you the outlook is great, because although you are over-fat, you have not become entangled in the failed dieter trap, and using this book gives you every chance of making significant and lasting fat loss without ever becoming involved in the vicious circle of conventional slimming diets.

Group B Basically Slim

Just as over-fat people may tend to under-estimate the size of their bodies, some groups of dieters fall into the opposite trap. They have an equally distorted body image – but in the opposite direction. While some over-fat people rarely look in a mirror without pulling in their tummies and standing on tip-toe, many people who are not over-fat see themselves as disgustingly rotund when they look in the mirror.

This group of people is basically slim, but diet repeatedly nevertheless – either because they regard themselves as fat even though they are not, or because they want to be still thinner even though they know they are not too fat. The basically slim can have just as much of a problem in facing how fat or thin they really are as genuinely fat people do. They can use similar yardsticks to help themselves towards a realistic knowledge.

Clothes again are an important test. If clothes hang off you; if you find it hard to get jeans that are not baggy; if people constantly comment on your slimness, then you are very unlikely to be over-fat. A journalist friend of mine used to diet and skip meals constantly in order to get slimmer, but at the same time she would come back from shopping trips moaning that she had been unable to find any clothes small enough to fit her. Why didn't they stock more size 8s (US size 4), she wailed. It took her a long time to see the contradiction between the two statements that she needed to diet and that clothes were too big for her.

Scale is also a problem. When you look in a mirror you see only yourself in isolation and there is no point of reference – another human being, or a whole roomscape for example. If you regularly look at yourself in a very small mirror you will be used to seeing yourself filling it, looking large, and you may be very surprised at the much smaller image if you happen to catch sight of yourself in, say, a large mirrored wall at a shopping centre. Try to catch yourself by surprise when you see yourself in a mirror – a quick glimpse of yourself reflected as you pass a shop window often reveals the true you.

If you are basically slim, it is vital to understand this and act on it. Examine the following basically slim categories for a more detailed insight.

Basically slim categories

• Habitual Dieter
If you fall into the Habitual Dieter category you are likely to be one of those people who always watches what they eat. Your friends envy your self-discipline although secretly they get bored with the fact that you never let up. Whether or not you see yourself as over-fat, you would probably describe yourself as always on a diet, and add that you dare not stop dieting in case you get fat or fatter. This is a tell-tale sign because it shows that deep inside, you admit to yourself that you are not really over-fat, so you have to justify your constant dieting with the idea that you might suddenly get over-fat for some reason.

Or maybe you *are* able to see yourself as not over-fat, and maybe not even likely to be over-fat, but nevertheless want to get thinner still. There is some very complicated psychology going on here and it is important that, with the help of the next chapter, you confront it because this category of dieter is at risk of acquiring eating disorders like anorexia.

• Naturally Slim

This lucky group of people – probably fewer than a quarter of the population – has never been over-fat and never dieted. The 'cheats' in this book are things that come instinctively to the naturally slim. For most of us the techniques I outline are what psychologists call 'learned behaviour' but for the naturally slim they are just unconscious habits. Behavioural psychologists believe that it takes about 100 days for a learned behaviour to become habitual, so if you consciously work at following the ideas in this book, within three months you will be well on the way to joining the group of naturally slim people. First, though, you have to know as much as possible about how they think, which will be discussed in the next chapter.

Group C Real Fluctuations in Fatness

Although most dieters tend to see life in terms of black or white – fat or thin – in fact, many of them fit into the group which the psychologists call 'bi-polar'. As the phrase implies, this group tends to swing from one end of the spectrum to the other. They can be rather over-fat and then lose that fat, perhaps through life changes or dieting, but regain it at a later period in their life. For some bi-polar fluctuators these swings can take place over short periods of time – within the space of a year or even a couple of months.

For others, though, the swings are long-term and can be more difficult to spot. Compare yourself with earlier periods in your life. Were you as plump while you were at school as you are now? Genuinely chronic obese people were usually the tubby ones at school. If you were like most of the rest of your form, pretty normal, then your present over-fat is part of a long-term fluctuation. Even if you were chubby as a child, that could have been a fat phase. Ask yourself if you are much fatter now than when you were a young adult – between the ages of 16 and 25. Do you wear a bigger clothes size than then? Ideally you should retain pretty much the same body shape as an adult that you had from the end of adolescence.

Many fluctuators recognise that their over-fatness goes up and down, but few face up to why this is happening. Look at the categories below to help your self-perception, and then have a serious think about the discussion of your problem in the next chapter.

Fluctuator categories

• Yo-Yo Dieter

Few diet writers distinguish between Failed Dieters and Yo-Yo Dieters, and yet it is vital to understand the differences in the outlook and experience of these two groups of people. Yo-Yo Dieters in fact are quite distinct from both Failed Dieters and Habitual Dieters. Since there are periods when the Yo-Yo Dieter is not over-fat, she certainly could not be regarded a true Failed Dieter. If you are a Yo-Yo Dieter it is likely that you have been on many different diets, but unlike the Habitual Dieter you are always ready to give up those diets and return to your original pattern of eating. Some Yo-Yo Dieters see the period between diets as an opportunity to over-eat, and like the Habitual Dieters they are at risk of eating disorders (especially bulimia). So if you fall into this category it is important to read more about it in Chapter Eight.

• Occasional Dieter

This more moderate version of the Yo-Yo Dieter is representative of a large proportion of the dieting population and is especially common among male dieters. The Occasional Dieter diets very rarely, but when he does he is moderately successful and the results are lasting. He will diet perhaps once a year for a specific reason – maybe after gaining over Christmas or to shape up for a holiday or sporting activity. Many women dieters find this laidback, yet essentially successful, approach frustratingly difficult to understand, so even if you are not an Occasional Dieter it will be helpful to read more about the type in the next chapter.

• Successful Dieter

This individual is someone who was genuinely over-fat but lost the fat through dieting and has maintained a new, stable, slim self for some years. This kind of dieter is rarer than hen's teeth. Nutritionists estimate that less than 10 per cent of the dieting population is in this category – some put the figure as low as one per cent. If you are in this category you've probably already published a book describing the diet that worked for you. What people forget, though, is that by definition, it won't work for 90 to 99 per cent of the rest of us. This is why successful dieters are surprisingly much less interesting to study from the would-be slimmer's point of view than people who are naturally slim.

CHAPTER EIGHT

I think, therefore I am slim

If you are a connoisseur of diet books – as many dieters are – you probably know the formula so well you could write one yourself. Here are some quotations from the opening passages of a few famous diet books:

- 'I have written this book, not because I believe it's better to be thinner, but because I have experienced the anguish of revolving my life around food.'
- 'I had two decades of feeling disgusted whenever I caught sight of my thighs but now that I live an anti-cellulite lifestyle I actually like them.'
- 'Ever since the author could remember she had suffered from an obsession with food, and sustained an almost life-long battle against obesity, resorting to desperate measures that more than once had landed her in hospital.'
- 'I looked awful in swimsuits, leotards and clingy clothes of all kinds.'
- 'My weight has yo-yo'd from 7 stone 12 pounds to over 10 stone but never ever have I been able to reduce my thighs to their present shape no matter how much weight I lost.'

All these passages have something in common – they explain that the author was once a fat person herself; that she struggled unsuccessfully for long periods of time to become slim; that eventually she became thin (or at least less fat) through following the diet she is about to describe to you.

These days starting a diet book this way is a tradition which many diet writers may feel obliged to adopt. The theory behind this – known as 'the testimonial' – is fairly simple and was much used by advertisers in the 50s and 60s to promote their products. An early commercial would run something like this: Harassed housewife extracts grey-looking laundry from washing machine with exasperated sigh. At this point thousands of equally harassed female viewers supposedly sympathise with her predicament. Then television housewife discovers new Whitewash and all her troubles are over. Female viewers rush out on cue to buy Whitewash themselves. The idea was that the buyer would identify strongly with her television counterpart and therefore believe in the testimonial provided by the fictional experience of the television pseudo-housewife.

In the last couple of decades, though, consumers have become much more cynical about commercials. They understand that the images held up for them to identify with are not real people at all, and they have spotted that all the products make the same claims regardless of their actual performance when bought and used. As present-day advertising techniques have had to become more sophisticated, we don't see the 'testimonial' style of commercial very much any more.

Why has the same degree of consumer awareness not developed with regard to diet books? Sadly the whole issue of thin and fat, of dieting and failing, is so clouded by emotion that it is very hard for those involved to see themselves as consumers (the very word has unpleasant associations); and the diet as a product. Instead there is an almost religious feel to the way the successful dieter – the convert – preaches her chosen diet creed to those who are still fat. If only we could overcome this and recognise that fat is not a matter of morality, and that a diet book is a manufactured product like any other, we would be able to make real progress in helping people to be healthier and happier. So let's start by looking at the issue of dieting and diet books from a logical point of view.

Why Dieting is Illogical

Is it a good idea to follow a particular diet because the author of the book propounding that diet claims it worked for them? Any statistician, nutritionist or indeed psychologist will answer that with a resounding 'No'. To start with, from a purely statistical point of view the odds are against you succeeding. We know that at least nine out of every 10 diets undertaken fail. So if we charitably assume that the diet writer is not lying when she says the diet worked for her, then the next nine people to follow that diet will fail. If the book sells 100,000 copies, best-seller level for diet books, then at least 90,000 people who buy the book will find that it does not work.

Even though that represents rather a lot of dissatisfied customers, there is another even more compelling reason for disregarding an author's diet testimonial – and that is the very existence of that testimonial itself. Crucially, it implies that the book has been written *from a standpoint of fatness*. The author is the first to stress this: she was fat, she writes, she is now thin. From the psychologist's point of view this statement marks out the author as a dieter, who is locked into the mentality of a dieter. Psychologists believe that any dieter, even a successful one, is probably still underlyingly a fat person. This is because the dieter is unable to shed the old attitudes to food – those of forbidden foods, or feast and famine, or food as something to be feared. Just as the reformed heavy drinker will always have a problem with alcohol, so the dieter will never have a completely relaxed relationship with food and their body. This is one reason so many successful dieters revert to their original obesity. Even nutritionists are now beginning to agree with this view – especially as far as it relates to the diet trap itself. Professor Phillip James, head of the WHO (World Health Organisation) International Obesity Task Force, recently told a conference: 'Telling people just to eat less is bonkers.' Nutritionist Susan Jebb was quoted in agreement with this: 'We don't want people to eat so little. The way to good health is to boost your energy requirement and change your exercise behaviour.'

Though logical, these views are not immediately obvious to those of us at the receiving end. We want to lose some fat, so we follow the advice of someone who has done so through dieting. What could be simpler? After 30 years or more as a dieting population, however, it is now beginning to be understood that fatness is a much more complex issue than we realised, and that overwhelmingly, dieting is an answer only for a minority of people.

The Psychology behind Dieting

As more research is done into this area, it is being recognised that the mindset leading to fatness is possibly even more important than the nutritional element. The major new theory in this area is that the psychology of the dieter is much closer to the psychology of the fat person than it is to that of the naturally thin person. Dr Deanna Jepson, an eating disorder specialist, says: 'You can be fit in the body but fat in the mind. If you think a certain way you will never feel safe. Food will be a constant temptation.' Which is why psychologists worry that the authors of diet books reflect the psychology of the dieter rather than that of the normally slim non-dieter.

If you want to discover the behaviour that leads to slimness, go to a slim person, not a dieter, argue the psychologists. This is such a logical idea, yet it really turns the present approach to fat loss on its head. Up until recently it had always been assumed that there was little to be learnt from naturally slim people simply because their behaviour was instinctive. Now we are being told that it is the successful dieters who have little relevance to us. Because their situation is so rare – less than 10 per cent of the dieting population – it just isn't applicable to the majority of us. But if a naturally slim person's behaviour is instinctive, then how can we learn from it? This is where a relatively new branch of psychology, cognitive therapy, has had an impact in the fight against fatness. This therapy has shown that people can take on new ways of thinking which are not instinctive to them, and that the new mindset can become as natural and habitual as was the old one. In other words, a fat person can learn to think like a thin person and eventually it will become second nature.

How to Think Thin

This is the most wonderful and dramatic cheat of all: you really can think yourself thin! If you can successfully acquire the mindset of a slim person, your attitudes – for example, towards food – will become those of a naturally slim person, and eventually you will become a naturally slim person yourself. How do we go about learning to think thin? Psychotherapy can help here too. Modern psychologists who study people's behaviour have found that outward behaviour can have a big effect on the inner psyche. Basically what they believe is that smiling even though you are feeling blue really does cheer you up.

These two therapy theories – cognitive and behavioural – are currently in widespread and very successful practice all over the world, dealing with a whole range of problems from career worries, to giving up smoking, to more serious psychiatric disorders. Their joint message is simple and positive: new, helpful habits of mind can be put into place; and they can be programmed into the mind initially just by copying and performing the right actions, even if the spirit isn't really in it to begin with. In fat-loss terms this means that if you watch the behaviour of a naturally slim person and copy it yourself, you will begin to develop their psychology; and eventually you will think like a slim person yourself.

This new way of looking at getting slim is a virtuous circle to replace the old vicious circle of the dieter. Here's what it looks like:

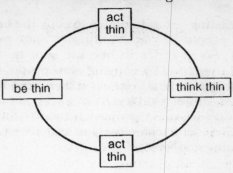

The great breakthrough here is the idea that your actions are not only determined by what you think, but that the converse is also true, namely that what you think can also be influenced by how you act. So the two elements reinforce each other constantly: act slim and you will think slim; think slim and you will continue to act slim. If you go through the motions of being a slim person for long enough – and psychologists have found that it takes about 100 days on average – then it will turn out that you are no longer pretending; you really are who you imagine you are.

In order to play the part of a thin person, you must first learn all about the psychology of slim, and how it differs from that of a fat person – and this is what this chapter will help you do.

HELENA CHRISTENSEN, supermodel

drinks a Sea Breeze – cranberry juice and vodka – for her favourite evening treat.

Thinking thin has almost nothing whatever to do with how you eat. Many people have assumed that to adopt the behaviour of a naturally slim person means eating less. This is the major misunderstanding behind dieting – that to diet is to copy the behaviour of slim people. In fact, naturally slim people do not diet. So in order to become slim by thinking yourself that way, by copying slim people, you will not need to diet. What you must do is get a thorough understanding of what it is that slim people are doing right – and what fat people and dieters are doing wrong. First let's look closely at exactly who is and isn't dieting and why.

DIETING PATTERNS OF SLIM AND FAT PEOPLE

	Group	Category	Characteristics	Approx. percentage of dieters
A	Basically slim	Naturally slim	does not diet	0 per cent
		Habitual dieter	diets constantly. Eating disorder: prone to anorexia	18 per cent
B	Genuinely over-fat	Failing dieter	diets constantly or repeatedly without success	40 per cent
		Chronic obese	does not diet. Eating disorder. Prone to compulsive eating	0 per cent
C	Real fluctuations in fatness	Yo-Yo dieter	alternately feasts and fasts, usually with corresponding changes in fatness. Eating disorder. Prone to bulimia	20 per cent
		Occasional dieter	diets once or twice per year for specific reasons with moderate success	12 per cent (more for men)
		Successful dieter	diets once with lasting success	1–10 per cent

From this table the major difference between naturally slim people and dieters becomes clear: dieters
use their dieting as a method of self-expression. This
is why there are so many different kinds of dieters,
dieting for so many different reasons and in so many
different ways. There are people who are basically
slim but diet anyway; there are people whose weight
goes up and down; and there are those who diet but
never get anywhere. Of course the slim people have
just as many problems in their lives, but these do
not figure on the table for one reason – they are not
expressed through dieting.

JACKIE AGYEPONG, Olympic hurdler

*'Before an event, food is the last thing you think
about.'*

Whatever a slim person's current hang-ups they
don't affect her attitude to food. If a slim person
suddenly has an overwhelming urge for a chocolate
eclair, for whatever reason, then she will go out and
buy precisely that, and eat it. If for some reason she
can't get hold of a chocolate eclair – her specific desire
– then she will be unlikely to eat a substitute. She
will simply have one if and when she can get one or
do without. To a dieter's psychology such a straightforward response would be impossible because her
attitude to food and the associations it carries for
her have become so complex.

> ## ELIZABETH HURLEY, model
>
> *'I allow myself the odd bar of chocolate and eat a
> packet of crisps every day. When I'm trying to lose
> weight, I cut out sugar altogether. Once you label
> a food "naughty" you automatically crave it, so if I
> feel like chocolate I eat it with no guilt. I can't stand
> low-fat food. I'd rather have one spoonful of delicious
> ice cream than huge amounts of tasteless stuff.'*

The most interesting difference is that the dieter – the
'fat' person – is actually less likely to end up eating
an eclair than the slim person. The dieter instantly
regards the desire for an eclair as something to
be controlled, whereas the slim person sees it as
something to be satisfied. If you have ever dieted
you will recognise the distinction immediately.

For example, a baby might think: 'want chocolate,
must have chocolate' but the subliminal message
going through a dieter's mind is: 'want chocolate,
must control myself'. Until recently most nutritionists and diet writers have assumed that the dieter
then fails to control herself and ends up eating the
chocolate anyway. It has been argued therefore that
failures of will-power are to blame for the inefficiency
of dieting, rather than any flaw in the basic theory
of dieting. In fact the newest research suggests that
most dieters do not lack will-power; that many of
them actually have far greater powers of self-control
than other groups of people. Food intake in this
country is down 20 per cent on what it was 10
years ago – largely due to dieters' ability to control
the amounts they eat.

Why Dieters are Control Freaks

Deanna Jepson has confirmed: 'Fat people are not weak-willed. They have trained themselves to go without food for as long as they can.' This new thinking flies in the face of the received view that fat people and failed dieters are inadequates whose lives and appetites are chaotically and constantly out of control. In fact, most dieters are super-controlled people. Calorie counters and the more recent fat-gram counters lead lives that border on the obsessive-compulsive, governed by charts and numbers and repeated counting exercises. Some habitual dieters have such great self-control over their appetites that they eventually become anorexic. Others alternate between periods of impossibly demanding self-denial and explosions of indulgence.

Deanna Jepson explains that when at last these people do get to eat they are too hungry to react normally. Really they are frightened of food and its implications. She says: 'They are food phobics.'

Can these be the same people normally regarded as loving food so much that they must control their desire to eat it? There are two elements at work here: food and control. Of these, control is just as important as food, yet almost no attention has been paid to it.

The truth of the matter is that dieters are far more addicted to control than they are to food. When we follow a diet we are told exactly what to eat and how much. Everything is laid out for us; there are no questions, just a promise of some vague future reward for self-denial now. It is nothing like real, adult life where virtue is rarely rewarded and every question has more than one answer. Looked at from this point of view it appears that failing and habitual dieters may indeed be getting exactly what they want from their dieting – but what they really want is not what we, and they, think they want. It is assumed they are dieting in order to look better. In fact, they may be dieting in order to be on a diet; that is, to have a control imposed on their lives.

The subconscious is very logical: what it wants is a sensation of being controlled; the diet provides that sensation. If dieting is successful then it is likely to be stopped, so the subconscious makes sure the diet never is successful either by undermining it so that it is not actually successful (failed diet; compulsive eating; binge/purge syndrome) or by not allowing it to be perceived as successful even when it is (anorexia).

Sociologists regard the desire to be under control as a form of evasion of personal responsibility. It is very much the 'jobsworth' attitude that says: 'I didn't want to do it, I was ordered to do it by someone else.' Seeking to impose artificial controls on yourself is a way of abnegating your free will. If you don't have free will then you don't have to take responsibility for your own actions and therefore you can escape the consequences of blame and guilt.

Dieting is full of these kinds of evasion. There is the binger's evasion that 'because I will diet tomorrow I have got permission to be irresponsible about food today'. You can eat, drink and be merry today, for tomorrow you diet. But the permission is totally dependent on the existence of the diet. If there is to be no diet tomorrow then responsibility must be taken now for today's eating and drinking – whether that means accepting the value of guilt-free enjoyment and personal gratification, or confronting the fact that self-gratification can get out of hand. Facing these issues and coming to terms with your response to them is something mature people do. Glossing over them by deflecting your thinking towards some unspecified future period is putting off being a grown-up person.

Extreme Dieters

Therapists working with extreme dieters – those with eating disorders – find these issues to be quite marked. They point out that taking responsibility for your eating might also mean taking responsibility for other areas of yourself and your life. Interestingly, there are some parallels here with people undergoing therapy for sex problems. For example some women have a rape fantasy – because sex is forced on them they have no guilt about it; they are not complicit in their enjoyment of sex. This has some similarities with dieters who fast and feast. The binge element of their behaviour is like the rape: they do not regard themselves as complicit because it is the severity of the previous fast which has driven them to it – their starvation has in a sense 'raped' them.

So dieters need to look quite carefully at what is really going on. Why might eating be dangerous or threatening? How do they really feel deep down about those complex issues of adulthood like free will, self-determination and responsibility? Is there perhaps something about themselves that means they don't want that inner self to be free from control? Are they truly confronting these issues or do they have a tendency to conceal them or avoid them?

This last question is particularly important, because it appears that most naturally slim, non-dieting people tend also to be natural confronters. Some of course do hide behind drink or other dysfunctional behaviours, but even these may be quite aggressive about confronting themselves – or equally often other people – with their fears and worries. Think of naturally slim, non-dieting, people you know and check out their behaviour against this table of slim characteristics compared with dieters' characteristics.

Non-Dieters		Dieters	
Flaws	Virtues	Flaws	Virtues
selfish	assertive	passive	often selfless
aggressive	confrontational	avoidant	placatory
impulsive	instinctive	controlling	likes to plan
neurotic, nervous, twitchy	energetic, dynamic	inactive	outwardly calm
impatient	lives in the present	lives in the future	looks ahead
talkers, not often good listeners	extroverted	tendency to agoraphobia	often good listeners
open, often reveal their problems	can be self-obsessed/boring	hides feelings	puts other people's feelings first
smokes/drinks	not afraid to gratify needs	suppresses needs	good provider for others
may be over-sexed	physical, tactile	distrustful of their physicality/body	caring

Non-dieter characteristics – both flaws and virtues – are generally regarded as pre-disposing people towards slimness, or helping over-fat people to become slim if they adopt some of them. Dieter attributes, whether good or bad, tend to trap people into patterns of failed dieting. People who display a combination of qualities, some non-dieter and some dieter, tend to be those whose behaviour would be regarded as paradoxical – that is, those who do not diet even though they are too fat, and those who do diet even though they are not too fat.

One of the most noticeable features of the chart is that many of the characteristics listed on the right-hand side are very often associated with women, while those on the left tend to be looked on as rather male qualities. For example, we see that dieters tend to be the sort of people who make good listeners, put other people's feelings first and are good providers. On the down side they can also have a tendency to be rather passive and not assertive enough. All these characteristics – good and bad – have been seen as stereotypically feminine.

By contrast, the non-dieters may often be aggressive, selfish, confrontational, impulsive and hyperactive, all things which society sees as male in origin. This may be one of the reasons why so many more women diet than men. It is estimated that at least three-quarters of our female population have been on a diet at some time or another, with probably half of them on a diet now or just about to start or finish one. Men, even nowadays, hardly diet at all. Yet the levels of mild and severe obesity are almost equal between the sexes. It may also explain why the few men who do diet often diet successfully – those male characteristics of aggression and self-assertion may help them to adapt their behaviour to that of slim, non-dieting people.

PALOMA PICASSO, designer

'I always look forward to a rucola, parmigiano, olive oil and ciabatta sandwich at Bar Amerini in Florence.'

The question of men and diets also highlights the point that not all people who don't diet are slim. Many over-fat people have never dieted, and these people tend to be 'combination personalities' – they have some non-dieter characteristics and some dieter characteristics. People who are over-fat through compulsive eating, for example, have an eating disorder just as valid as bulimia or anorexia. Compulsive eaters often display attributes of avoidance, suppression of needs and hyper-caringness that are associated with dieting. Yet they may combine these features with the non-diet characteristics of being rather extroverted, somewhat aggressive and impulsive.

Habitual Dieters

Another combination personality is that of the habitual dieter – really the flip side of the compulsive eater. Where the compulsive eater is fat but doesn't diet, the habitual dieter is thin but does diet. The habitual dieter will display some non-dieter characteristics (which helped her to be slim in the first place) like dynamism, energy and activity; but she will also have many dieter attributes (which compel her to keep dieting) such as being a good listener, being selfless, suppressing her needs.

The Princess of Wales makes an interesting case study of this kind of dieter. Although she has had brief periods of mild bulimia, her overall profile is that of the habitual dieter. Though never genuinely over-fat (her engagement photographs show a physique completely normal for a 19-year-old girl) she has dieted habitually since her marriage. Her universally recognised virtues – her ability to listen to the problems of others and empathise with them, and her qualities as a mother – are typically those of a dieter. On the other hand she has often been criticised as self-obsessed, impulsive and a self-dramatist: all flaws common to naturally slim non-dieters. This combination personality profile is just what you would expect of the slim dieter, just as combination personalities are prevalent among fat non-dieters.

In recent years, however, another side of Diana has come to the fore, characterised by a more positive form of assertiveness and a new-found ability to confront her problems. These are non-dieter virtues, as opposed to flaws, and it seems likely that the mature Diana will have given up habitual dieting.

Looking at these combination personalities makes it easy to see why fatness and dieting are such complex issues, and why the sort of blanket answers so often offered are rarely adequate. By understanding exactly where your own personality fits in, you will be able to develop a much more successful approach to solving your problems. From the self-assessment on page 221 you should now be able to give a name to your own particular group of fatness and diet issues. You may be like Princess Diana, a Habitual Dieter who is not really too fat but continues to flirt with diets all the same. Or perhaps you are a Failed Dieter, repeatedly fighting a losing battle against over-fat. Maybe you are a Yo-Yo Dieter, like the Duchess of York, and you wish you could maintain a slim figure permanently. Whatever your category, it is now time to look at a detailed analysis of the psychology behind it – and to discover the thin-thinking tricks you can use to overcome it.

Failing Dieter

Analysis

This group covers about 40 per cent of dieters, making it the most common category. Failing Dieters have almost no non-dieter characteristics in their personality and are often seen by others as having excellent feminine caring qualities. Their good points are their selflessness, their desire to provide for and nurture others, and their general tendency to put others first. The opposite side of the same coin, though, is that they are not assertive enough; they suppress their own needs; they avoid facing up to their inner feeling and problems.

Failing Dieter Case History

Jenny is a middle-aged mother whose children have flown the nest, leaving her feeling lonely, functionless and depressed. She has had an over-fat problem ever since her first pregnancy and though she has been on many diets it has always been difficult to stick to them because it means making different meals for her and the family, and she always seems to end up eating left-overs anyway. At the moment she has even gained a little more because she is tending to eat to cheer herself up.

Diagnosis: Jenny has always put herself and her needs second to her family. Now that those family needs are no longer pressing, Jenny is being forced to confront herself and her own needs. Because she has avoided this for so long, she now feels lost, confused and fearful.

Answers

1 Get in touch with your needs

If ever there was a case for the old feminist cliché of 'consciousness raising' it is that of the Failed Dieter. Discovering how to be more assertive – even aggressive – and perhaps a little selfish from time to time will make a huge difference. Start by buying yourself a big diary or exercise book.

To begin with, use it to record your feelings day to day – especially times when you didn't put yourself first. For example, maybe you missed your favourite TV programme in order to collect your husband from the station but it turned out that he took a later train. Note down how you felt – angry, probably – and how you behaved. Perhaps you excused your husband by assuming he had been working late, and served dinner as usual, consoling yourself with an extra helping. Write down that you felt angry – go on, admit it.

DENISE LEWIS, Olympic heptathlete

'I've been doing meditation and visualisation for about three years now. It makes you more aware of yourself and gives you an inner confidence.'

Keep your 'feelings diary' like this for a few weeks and then look back over it. Did you often feel put upon? Have you written down feelings that you wouldn't have dared say out loud? Don't panic, you won't have to express those feelings. The next stage is to look at the various incidents and work out how things could have been different so you wouldn't have felt that way in the first place. For example – the wasted journey to the station. Realise that next time your husband needs you to pick him up and it clashes with something you want to do, there are alternatives.

You could book a taxi to meet him; or you could ask your driving son or daughter to do it; or you could think of a neighbour who might be able to help. Best still, if it's not too far, you could do him the favour of suggesting he walk – everybody can benefit from an extra exercise opportunity.

At first this is going to seem very radical, but assertive people do it all the time without even thinking about it. Doing it successfully just once is all it takes to discover how well it works and how much better it makes you feel – without upsetting people around you. When you've got the hang of this, you can start using your diary for forward planning as well as retrospective analysis. Schedule time in your diary that is purely for you, to take some kind of positive step that will answer a particular need.

For most Failed Dieters, a major need will be to feel and look slimmer – which is why there are plenty of make-over tips in this book. But it only works if you actually do it. Mary Spillane, the British founder of the Color Me Beautiful image consultancy, stresses: 'Lots of these quick, easy little tricks like changing your clothing or getting your colours done by a professional will work overnight. It is by doing some of these instant result things that you discover you are really worth it – and that you deserve to be good to yourself.' If doing these things feels selfish or aggressive to you, don't worry – just do them anyway, that's what a thin thinker would do.

2 Take action now

Whatever you decide to do, equally important is doing it now. Failed Dieters have a great tendency to put their life on hold. They think: I'll buy myself a new dress/join the gym/get out more/tell the boss to get stuffed . . . when I'm slimmer. Of course they never do become slimmer. From the information in this chapter you can now realise that the very reason somebody like this doesn't succeed in becoming slimmer is because it would mean actually doing all those things. Underneath it all, the prospect of doing those assertive, self-nurturing things is frightening. So Failed Dieters undermine themselves in every way: by not doing things to improve their morale in the present, they remain passive; by keeping the sub-conscious threat of doing those things in the future, they torpedo their efforts to get slim.

JANINE DI GIOVANNI, foreign correspondent

'Although I have always prided myself on my ability to survive in hostile environments like Bosnia, Liberia and Rwanda I was terrified when I went designer boutique shopping for a party dress. I now know which designers work for me and which don't. I opt for clothes that contain Lycra.'

One fairly painless way out of this vicious circle is to have a make-over. This gets right to the heart of the problem by showing you that you can look good now, not later, but today, the real you. Mary Spillane says: 'If you get things noticed immediately it is a great morale booster. It can also be very revealing. I was called in on a television diet and exercise programme where there was no time to do before and after shots of the guinea pigs. So they photographed them and then I made them over for the after shot. They all looked convincingly as if they had been dieting and exercising for at least a month – which just goes to show!'

3 Any change is good change

Many Failed Dieters are actually too afraid of changing to allow themselves to achieve change – another reason why their diets are doomed, as successful diet would mean change. But psychologists insist that if you are in a situation that isn't working for you, any change will be a change for the better. Hold this thought while you are reviewing what is wrong in your life and trying to discover the things you are afraid of changing. For example, are you subconsciously afraid that being a slim person would mean being a different person? Perhaps the sort of person you think you or your family might not like? Only you can supply the answers to these questions.

4 Shine at something

Because they have repressed their own needs for so long, self-esteem is a big problem for failed dieters. You will notice that a lot of the advice in this book centres on being more confident about who you are and what you are about. It could basically be summed up as: 'Stop sitting at home thinking about food; get out there and have a good time.' For Failed Dieters the main point of this is that it gives the opportunity to enjoy life, and this in turn helps to raise self-esteem. Mary Spillane says: 'It is how you feel about yourself that determines how people will react to you.' So find chances for yourself to do things you enjoy doing and are good at, and your confidence will improve.

RACHEL HUNTER, model

'Kick-boxing has given me more confidence. Modern women have changed so much in the last 20 years. They have to cope with such a lot and need an outlet for stress, which kick-boxing can give you.'

Habitual Dieter

Analysis

As we have seen, the Habitual Dieter is someone who is not over-fat, but diets all the same. To someone who is not a Habitual Dieter, this behaviour can be very hard to understand. The Failed Dieter, for example, often has a lunching companion who is an Habitual Dieter. The Failed Dieter looks on in misery as the Habitual Dieter picks at her food before eventually pushing it away declaring herself to be watching her weight. 'And she's not even fat,' thinks the Failed Dieter, as she loses the strug-gle against temptation. If the Failed Dieter were to become successful in changing her own behaviour she would let her anger show by telling the Habitual Dieter to pull herself together and get a life, before deciding not to lunch with her any more. This would help the Failed Dieter, but not the Habitual Dieter who is in fact just as unhappy.

Many readers will probably not believe that it is possible to be slim and unhappy. Part of the problem is that many Habitual Dieters do not see themselves as slim. They have both a distorted body image and low self-esteem and therefore regard themselves as obese and disgusting even if in reality they have an ideal figure. When pressed Habitual Dieters may admit that they can logically work out that they are not fat, for example from their dress size, but they still see themselves as disgusting and since obesity is currently regarded as disgusting, they must be obese.

A slight variation on this line of thinking comes among the perfectionist Habitual Dieters who can recognise that they have a satisfactory figure, but still believe it could be better. Although they cannot admit it to themselves they are looking toward dieting to cure dissatisfactions in other areas – to make them more successful, wealthier, taller.

For all Habitual Dieters though, the need for control is a dominant characteristic, she is what Americans would call a control freak. She has become obsessed with imposing an outward order and discipline on her life, and by being so all-consuming this obsession gives her an excuse for failing to engage with the real issues that are making her dissatisfied, unhappy or even fearful.

Fortunately the healthy human psyche has its own ways of overcoming obsession, so that very few Habitual Dieters ever do become mono-maniac enough to pursue their illogic to its ultimate conclusion. However, some do, and these are the people most at risk of the eating disorder anorexia. It is interesting to note that many recovered anorexics, looking back at the time they teetered over the brink from dieting into anorexia, recall their initial pleasure in dieting as being the one area of their life of which they were fully in control.

Though anorexics will find much that is useful in this book, theirs is a serious medical problem for which professional help should be sought.

Habitual Dieter Case History

Nicola is an attractive and successful young career woman. She was always reasonably slim at school and college and had never dieted or bothered much about her figure until she started working in retailing. Now though, she weighs herself constantly and is desperate to get down to under 8 stone (50kg). She feels her appearance is very important to her career and is terrified that she might put on weight. Others think of her as an extremely well-groomed, fashionable young woman; but she longs to look like the models and celebrities she sees on television and in magazines.

Diagnosis: Nicola lacks self-esteem and this makes it easy for her to sublimate her very natural concerns about her career into an obsession with her weight. She is looking towards a diet to make her feel less worried and happier with herself.

Answers

1 Grow Up

This advice may sound abrupt but it is important for the Habitual Dieter to recognise that her symptoms are associated with immaturity. Having compulsions, neuroses and hang-ups over food is a sign of emotional ill-health. Onlookers who don't know it actually recognise it subconsciously. We all hate faddy eaters and Californian-style eating.

Conversely, eating healthily in public is good; it is a sign of maturity. Men like watching women eat – eating is sexy. Habitual Dieters tend to be fairly intelligent, so now it is time to turn some of your brain power to this area. Make a conscious effort to analyse the behaviour of people around you – especially non-dieters. Are they more tolerant than you, more open to new ideas, generally broad-minded? These are all attributes of genuinely mature people and adopting them might help you to become more accepting of yourself. Try to question your own behaviour more and be realistic about whether you may be unnecessarily tense or poor at handling stress.

2 Nurture Self-Esteem

Although outwardly they look in control, so well-groomed and self-assured, many Habitual Dieters have very low self-esteem. They may be highly competitive and perfectionist and constantly create new standards by which they can regard themselves as failing. An Habitual Dieter who achieves a long-desired promotion will not allow herself time to bask in glory; instead she will immediately start comparing herself with her new boss.

It is important that the Habitual Dieter does make space for a few moments' self-celebration every now and then. It might help to have an 'ego wall' where you put up all your certificates and memorabilia of successful times in your life. Even if your achievements are less tangible you can still remind yourself of them – perhaps when you are preparing to go out. For an Habitual Dieter these areas of positive proof of self-worth are vital to armour yourself against the creeping assault on your self-esteem which will probably always plague you.

3 Confront Issues

Perhaps the most important thing for the Habitual Dieter to do is confront underlying reasons behind her continued dieting. She should ask herself why control is such an important element in her life. What things are so threatening that she wants to avoid them? Are there underlying fears in her life? Why is taking responsiblity for her eating and her behaviour such a worrying prospect? These are questions that we all need to ask ourselves at some point in our lives if we are successfully to complete the journey to full adulthood. Some of us are able to arrive at the answers without too much soul-searching; others need therapy to help them; and many never even ask. An Habitual Dieter – a slim person who is continuing to punish herself through dysfunctional eating – must recognise that she has much to gain from confronting these issues.

JULIA ROBERTS, actress

uses boxercise to work out and release stress at the same time.

Yo-Yo Dieter

Analysis

As the name implies, the Yo-Yo Dieter is someone whose level of fatness is constantly fluctuating. She will diet down to her ideal figure – or she may even get to the stage of being too thin – then she will let go all discipline and indulge herself until she is once more genuinely over-fat. A typical sign of a Yo-Yo Dieter is having two wardrobes of clothes – one for thin periods and one for fat periods.

Most Yo-Yo Dieters create this pattern through alternately feasting and fasting. Although they do not diet constantly like Failing and Habitual Dieters, it seems that they need the prop of being on a diet just as much. As soon as they reach a level at which they no longer need to get slim, they immediately start to get fat again. Their behaviour demonstrates that they are not thinking thin, even though they may at times be slim.

A more severe form of the syndrome is that of bulimia. Unlike true Yo-Yo Dieters, bulimics tend to remain at roughly the same level of fatness the whole time. This is because they have telescoped the whole cycle of feasting and fasting into a much shorter time scale. While a Yo-Yo Dieter's feast-fast cycle can take place over months or even years, for a bulimic it can happen in a matter of hours. The bulimic will wolf down any and every food she can lay her hands on – and it is a characteristic of bulimics to eat with their hands – then she will vomit the partially digested food. In severe cases this vomiting is more like simple regurgitation.

> *Bulimia is a serious medical problem, and sufferers should seek professional help.*

Yo-Yo Dieter Case History

Jemima is in her late twenties and first dieted when she was at boarding school and everybody did it. She had a bit of puppy fat then anyway and it was great to get really thin. But when she started work there was a lot of socialising and she was very soon unable to fit into her clothes. During a bad dose of flu though, she couldn't eat anything for a week. At the end of it she felt wonderfully thin and ever since then she has alternated between times of nearly starving herself and periods of total indulgence. Jemima has two sets of clothes for her thin times and her fat times.

Diagnosis: Jemima has fallen into the trap which catches many dieters – going below her natural weight and then rebounding back above it. By constantly regaining weight she is subconsciously setting herself the challenge of losing it again and this may be symptomatic that she is not challenged enough in other areas of her life. She may be under-achieving.

Answers

1 Learn to Accept

The single most important thing that the Yo-Yo Dieter can do to get out of her predicament is to learn self-acceptance. At its most basic level that can be something as simple as revising your ideal weight up by half a stone, or better still, stopping weighing yourself at all. One recovered Yo-Yo Dieter described how successful her change in goal had been: 'My GP says my new weight is perfectly healthy. I feel well. I'm reasonably fit. I'm sticking where I am because I can live with it.' These relaxed and laidback statements are very far from the Yo-Yo Dieter's normal state of eating tension.

> ### NIGELLA LAWSON, columnist
>
> *'I can actually eat quite a lot, whereas if I were still aiming for the 8½ stone [54 kg] I struggled to be throughout my early twenties, I'd eat a pea and put on weight.'*

Another good way to encourage self-acceptance is to abandon the 'third wardrobe' fallacy so common to Yo-Yo Dieters. This is the wardrobe of clothes they never wear because they never actually get skinny enough to fit them – the other two of course are for fat times and normal times. Mary Spillane is fairly severe about this: 'If you are not likely to get into it, throw it out. Don't have three different wardrobes. Just get clever, girl. You wouldn't believe the number of women I meet in business who tell me they never take their jacket off because the stomach is bulging out. And it stops the circulation. So get real.'

2 Stop repressing

Most categories of dieters have some underlying issues which their dieting is helping them to avoid confronting. Eating disorder specialists suggest that Yo-Yo Dieters are probably more repressive than most, and that the feelings they are repressing may be violent, angry or frustrated. Try to be a little introspective and identify what it is you might be repressing. If you find this difficult, there are many ways of getting help. Apart from professional psychotherapists, there are voluntary counsellors and self-help groups aimed at helping people with even mild eating disorders. To get in touch with these look in local phone directories or Yellow Pages, or ask your doctor or health club.

3 Have an affair

This may sound flippant, but often a flirtation like a holiday romance or some similar adventure is all the Yo-Yo Dieter needs to jerk her out of her feasting/fasting syndrome. As we have discovered, Yo-Yo Dieters tend to be underlyingly bored or unfulfilled. Embarking on a new relationship – or friendship – can provide healthy stimulation, thus fulfilling the need for excitement. Or go further still, and try the ideas below.

> **VERONICA WEBB, model, TV presenter**
>
> *'I'm the sort of girl who thinks falling in love and dancing are easily the best ways to keep thin.'*

4 Start something new

For Yo-Yo Dieters, starting some new venture – whether professionally or as a hobby – can be very helpful because it gives them a new forum to express themselves which isn't food. Mary Spillane experienced that herself when she started the British arm of Color Me Beautiful: 'When I started the business here in the UK everyone said it was stupid and the idea of going to someone as an image consultant was dismissed. Thirteen years later we are now doing it for Marks and Spencer. With things like that, all of a sudden life opens up. I have found that American women are much more open to this. They will give it a go and say I am worth it. British women could learn from that.'

TERI HATCHER, actress

lost nearly a stone through sheer hard work on filming the re-vamped series of New Adventures of Superman

---

Occasional Dieter

The Occasional Dieter really needs little advice from this book. He is one of the very few people for whom dieting is not an emotional issue. To him, both consciously and sub-consciously, a diet fulfils no other purpose than to shift a small amount of excess fat. He diets for a week or so once or twice a year for a specific reason. Maybe he wants to deal with a little post-Christmas bulge, or get down to fighting weight for the rugby season, or look better on the beach on holiday. Whatever it is, he will usually have his own patent method that has worked on previous occasions. These may include giving up drinking for a fortnight; cutting out fat; giving up second helpings; stopping business lunches for a few weeks; going vegetarian for a while.

The Occasional Dieter is really very close to being a naturally slim person. Certainly he doesn't imbue his eating or lack of it with any special significance. Generally Occasional Dieters tend to be men, for the same reasons that many non-dieters are male. However there are women who are well-balanced enough to take this approach to eating as well, although they may have reached this happy state only after long struggles with one or more of the dieting syndromes and by making a real effort to gain self-knowledge.

There is little to be said about Occasional Dieters here, because the whole thrust of this book is really about turning dieters into Occasional Dieters. But for those who are already naturally Occasional Dieters, one thing to consider might be increasing exercise levels in order to prevent those occasional peaks occurring at all.

Chronic Obese

Although the Chronic Obese person may seem totally different from our ideal of the Naturally Slim person, in fact they have much in common. Even though one group is fat and the other thin, they are the only two categories which do not diet and have never dieted. This means that the Chronic Obese person in all probability shares many character traits with the Naturally Slim person, which should help them to become slim should they ever want to. But the most important characteristic of the Chronic Obese person is that they do not want to become slim; it is simply not a priority. Should it ever become so, the issues facing the Chronic Obese person can become more complex.

It may turn out they are one of those rare people in whom there really is a 'thin person just waiting to come out'. Once they try to become less fat, they succeed and remain permanently slim. Often these people are those ectomorphic individuals whom everybody thinks of as tall and big with it, but underneath are really tall and skinny. This kind of successful slimmer frequently loses their excess fat through lifestyle change or commencing exercise, rather than through dieting. For people like these, who don't have any underlying hang-ups about food, losing fat is a fairly simple matter, easily achieved with a little advice from the local health club, gym or the family doctor.

Other Chronic Obese people who decide to try to become slimmer find that they have difficulties, and these can be grouped among those people discussed earlier in this chapter who have a combination of both non-dieter and dieter characteristics in their make-up. Once they attempt a diet they may discover that their eating is in fact compulsive. Compulsive eaters have even less chance than the rest of us of losing fat through dieting. They have the non-dieter's traits of extroversion, impatience and aggression which lead them to reject dieting; but they also have the dieter's problems of suppression of personal needs, hyper-caringness and avoidance which draw them to depend on food. Though rarely recognised as such, compulsive eating is an eating disorder just as much as bulimia and anorexia.

There is much in this book to help compulsive eaters, but there is no substitute for professional guidance.

CONCLUSION

Who Do You Think You're Cheating?

Every time we go on a new diet we are avoiding living now, in the real, present world. The underlying message of that Monday morning diet is: 'Today, as I presently am, I am unacceptable, therefore I will go on a diet so that at some time in the future – next week, the week after – I will be a slimmer, better person.' We are putting off accepting ourselves, and we are denying ourselves a pile of other positive attributes – those of liking ourselves, believing in ourselves, giving ourselves the power to get on and do things now. In writing this book I wanted to show my readers that it doesn't have to be this way. Changing the way you look is fairly superficial, but it is a start, and one that can be accomplished so easily. I want my readers to see that if they can stop the negativity in just this one area of their lives, then so much will follow.

That means thinking about what is possible now, in reality. Of course we could all be supermodels at some mythical time in the future – but that's all it is, a myth. Fantasy is fun, but reality is better. I think it is healthier to set your heart on something that is really achievable, and right for you as an individual, than to fixate on dreams that have little or no chance of coming true. If you have experienced the fulfilment that comes from actually achieving a goal, no matter how limited, you will understand just how confident

and powerful it makes you feel. The Americans call
it 'empowerment' and I like the phrase, though we
less jargon-prone British would probably describe it
as 'the art of the possible'.

Whatever you want to call it – cheating; not putting
your life on hold; living in the now – this book is
about freeing yourself from the tyranny of dieting
and all that it implies. So, whether you are size 8
or 28, you have a right to be yourself. Relish your
individuality: go out there and fill that you-sized
space in the world.

Further Reading

Andes, Karen, *A Woman's Book of Strength* (Perigee, 1995)

Bean, Anita, and Wellington, Peggy, *Sports Nutrition for Women* (A&C Black, 1996)

Celin, Dr John, *Cosmetic Surgery and Skin Care* (Celin, 1996)

Colgan, Dr Michael, *Optimum Sports Nutrition* (Advanced Research Press, 1993)

Dancy, Dr Elisabeth, *The Cellulite Solution* (Coronet Books, 1996)

Mervyn, Leonard, *Thorsons' Complete Guide to Vitamins and Minerals* (Thorsons, 1989)

Orbach, Susie, *Fat is a Feminist Issue* 2 (Hamlyn, 1984)

Reynolds, Bill, and Jayde, Negrita, *Sliced* (Contemporary Books, 1992)

Wells, Christine, *Women, Sport and Performance* (Human Kinetics, 1985)

Useful Addresses

Anna Daniels Fitness, Tunbridge Wells, Kent
Tel: 01892 783398

Association of Teachers of Pilates-Based Body Awareness, 182 Shaftesbury Avenue, London, WC2H 8JJ
Tel: 0171 240 5922

Color Me Beautiful Image Consultants, Freepost, London, SW8 3BR
Tel: 0171 627 5211

Elliot Lancaster, personal trainer, Christchurch, Bournemouth
Tel: 01202 481571

Fitness Professionals, UEL, Longbridge Road, Dagenham, Essex, RM8 2AS
Tel: 0990 133 434

Peter Van Minnen, Body Stress Release Practitioner, Neal's Yard Therapy Rooms, 2 Neal's Yard, Covent Garden, London, WC2H 9DP
Tel: 0171 379 7662

Solgar Vitamins, Solgar House, Chiltern Commerce Centre, Asheridge Road, Chesham, Bucks, HP5 2PY
Tel: 01494 791691

The Association of Pilates Teachers, 17 Queensberry Mews West, London, SW7 2DY
Tel: 0171 581 7041

The Exercise Association, The National Governing Body for Exercise and Fitness
Tel: 0171 278 0811

Index